PREFACE

If you want to learn more about your favorite water, or learn about other overlooked hotspots in this region, **Larry Larsen's Guide to South Florida Bass Waters** is for you.

If your favorite water is not mentioned, there could be several reasons:

1. The author is not aware of the productivity of your favorite spot;

2. With so many waters to cover, it is impossible to mention each and every one;

3. The author may be keeping it a secret for himself. Other reasons might be that the water is too small and heavy fishing pressure could devastate it, or it's private, or it's currently not known to be productive. Finally, it may simply be located in a different region, so check the other books in this series.

This book should be a reference source for all anglers who fish or wish to fish in the future the waters of South Florida. This region has three of the state's five largest lakes; two are remote and one is lightly pressured. All offer excellent bass fishing.

Each chapter focuses on the "name" lakes and rivers in the region that almost always produce good bass fishing and on many overlooked waters that quietly produce good bass fishing as well. The places mentioned in each chapter are waters where you can usually catch largemouth bass. Those waters where sunshine (hybrid striped bass) and peacock bass are available are also noted.

Additionally, productive methods that will help the reader catch more and larger bass on these particular waters are presented in **Larry Larsen's Guide To South Florida Bass Waters**. The proven techniques, lures and baits discussed within the pages of this book should help you be better prepared to tackle one of the rivers or lakes in the book on your next time out.

CONTENTS

The author has caught big bass from hundreds of lakes and rivers in South Florida. For the past 24 years, Larry has covered the state in his quest for great bass waters. Fishing more than 1,000 of Florida's lakes and rivers qualify him to author the Guide to Florida Bass Waters series of books. His Florida fishing success includes numerous bass between five and 12 pounds from the waters mentioned.

INTRODUCTION

THE GUIDE AND YOUR GUIDE

Learn everything there is to know about your next South Florida bass fishing destination and your trip will be better planned and more productive. **Guide To South Florida Bass Waters** is your best resource for trip planning, seasonal information, water characteristics and other interesting and necessary details that will make your bass fishing trip less of a guessing game.

Guide To South Florida Bass Waters focuses on the top bass rivers and lakes from Brevard County in the east coast to Polk and Osceola Counties, and west to Manatee County and south to the sawgrass canals of South Florida and the Everglades. This region has three of the state's five largest lakes; two are remote and one is lightly pressured. All offer excellent bass fishing and beautiful scenery at the same time.

To help you better locate productive spots, the book lists specific locations on each of the waters covered, and effective techniques that the author and other expert bass guides and professional fishermen have employed. Launching areas, maps and other lake details are also included for many of the region's lakes and rivers. Largemouth bass are the main focus of this book, yet peacock bass and hybrid striper bass (sunshine bass) are also mentioned when the opportunity exists for a significant catch on a specific body of water.

The specific waters within these pages were picked because they are consistently productive for numbers or bass, and/or because they produce lunker-size largemouth. These waters are also popular, with a local reputation for quality fisheries, and are

7

accessible to most anglers with canoes, johnboats or larger bass boats.

Some of the most interesting and valuable aspects of **Guide to South Florida Bass Waters** are the seasonal information, lures and tackle recommendations, and detailed locations mentioned for improving the angler's bass catching success. The author, Larry Larsen, takes the time to outline specific locations in lakes, rivers and creeks, information that is normally not possible to include in many magazine articles due to lack of space.

It is improbable at least that readers would not learn something from Larry's knowledge and experience. An award-winning author of over a dozen other books on bass fishing, few writers are more qualified and knowledgeable about Florida's bass waters. He enjoys Florida bass fishing as much as he enjoys writing about it, and he's as good an angler as he is a writer.

Over the past eight years, Larry has covered the state for Outdoor Life as their Florida Editor, fishing and writing about the top waters and those often overlooked. His numerous articles on Florida bass waters have also appeared in Florida Sportsman, and many other regional and national publications.

Guide to South Florida Bass Waters is the third of the Bass Waters Series which also includes North Florida and Central Florida Bass Waters. The book includes several appendices that an informed reader should find of interest. Appendix A lists the significant lakes and rivers in each South Florida county and the surface acreage of each. The addresses and telephone numbers of the game and fish office and those of the county chambers of commerce are listed in Appendix B.

To help broaden your knowledge on fresh and salt water fishing, and hunting, Appendix C is the informative Fishing & Hunting Resource Directory. A compilation of quality outdoor reference books that are extremely popular with sportsmen is presented.

Information on how to obtain the most comprehensive maps for many of the state's lakes is also available in Appendix D.

Finally, the comprehensive Index includes a cross reference of lakes, cities, bass species, counties and fisheries information that will help you quickly locate and review each reference throughout the book.

I'm sure you will enjoy learning from Larry's expertise, as I have over the years. -- Lilliam M. Larsen

1

LAKE TOHO - GIANT PRODUCER

THE BEST LARGEMOUTH water in the state is normally Lake Tohopekaliga, according to most creel surveys by the Game and Fresh Water Fish Commission. In fact, the annual survey usually reveals that Lake Tohopekaliga, better known as just "Toho," is in its prime during the fall months, when the average catch is twice the state average.

In an average Florida lake, it takes about four hours to catch a keeping-size bass, according to the Commission. That's a fishing success rate of .25 largemouth per hour. Toho produces about .50 bass per hour of fishing. Anglers haul in a keeper every two hours here, according to those statistics. My experience on this lake confirms those figures.

The perennial giant producer in the South is Lake Tohopekaliga.

I've liked West Lake Tohopekaliga since I first dropped my bass rig into its tannic-stained waters. That was in 1968 and the fishing there over the past 24 years has always been kind to me. The fishery has not escaped its share of problems throughout the years, but few other bodies of water have the resilience of Toho. Too, my "luck" on the lake is difficult to comprehend sometimes.

Imagine a small 40-boat club tournament held on the lake in the early 70's. The one-day event sponsored by a Melbourne bass club was actually tough fishing for most. Fortunately, I had located some bass early and had my seven fish club limit within an hour and a half of "blast off." I caught 26 pounds of largemouth and bested my second-place partner with 15 pounds, and the rest of the field, by a very wide margin.

A few years later I was encouraged to enter a state tournament being held on Toho. I wasn't sure the long drive from Jacksonville was worth it, so I went as a "non boater." Fishing from the back seat of the boat belonging to a pro angler, I caught a 9 1/2 pounder, a six pounder and one just over three pounds on as many successive casts within an hour of "blast off." From that point on, the tournament day was a real pleasure. My partner eventually caught a few fish, and I caught several more. I won that event easily.

That action took place in the shallow flats of bulrush and maidencaine that are so abundant on the shallow lake in Osceola County. On many other occasions since then, I've found bass of all sizes to be extremely cooperative. They usually seem to know when I'm coming and have a desire to show me a good time.

I was doing an assigned article for one of the national outdoor magazine on guide Wayne Yohn (my book "Bass Guide Tips" details how he catches giants from Toho). The Toho expert and I had one morning to develop the story, shoot the required pictures and of course, catch the bass. Writers aren't always so lucky to accomplish all objectives in an abbreviated trip, but I was that day.

Wayne and I were on the water at around 9 a.m. Within two hours, we each had two largemouth, and his were definite "picture-fish" quality. One weighed over ten pounds and the other weighed a very respectable 6 1/2 pounds. We weighed the fish at a marina prior to photographing and then releasing them. Those fish were taken by flippin' worms to the dense vegetation!

Lake Toho has been able to maintain a healthy fishery over the years that I've been fishing it, thanks to extreme drawdowns that have occurred at eight year intervals since 1971. Slightly less than half of the vegetated zone was exposed each time and bottom sediments and undesirable weed growth were reduced. Introduction of native plants helped to restore the lake's health.

TROPHY BASS CAPITAL

John Faircloth caught the healthiest Lake Toho bass in 1986. The lake record largemouth was caught on an eight-inch worm from the mouth of Shingle Creek in the hottest month of the year, July. It weighed 17 pounds, 12 ounces. The hot-weather catch proved that monster bass can be taken during months other than when the big female largemouth are initiating their spawning activities. Catching a giant Lake Toho bass when it is not full of roe probably offers future generations a better chance.

The variety of vegetation on Lake Tohopekaliga is tremendous habitat for giant largemouth.

The Kissimmee resident was casting the "Texas-rigged" Tequila Sunrise-colored worm with 1/16-ounce slip sinker and 4/0 hook from the bank toward the opposite shoreline. Faircloth knew where the big fish was hiding out in the stained waters, since he had lost it just one week earlier. The giant bass had broken the rod then and escaped. This time the fish wasn't so lucky.

The angler had just begun his "yo-yo" retrieve pulling the worm through the eight-foot depths when the bass hit. The worm, consisting of several fat body segments, large egg sack, two serrated curl arms, and a long serrated curl tail, provided the fish a with mouthful. The angler fought the monster bass for approximately 20 minutes on 14-pound test Trilene monofilament as the fish tried to dive into the cypress snags present.

The 28-inch long catch was in excellent physical shape. There was speculation that Faircloth's largemouth, with an additional year of growth, might have had a legitimate shot at the 20-pound 2-ounce state record during spawning season when full of roe. The lake record is a giant catch from any water, but Toho seems to produce more than its share. Trophy bass in the 14 and 15-pound class and a 20-fish stringer weighing 148.23 pounds caught by a husband and wife back in 1977 have been taken from the lake. In South Florida, Toho is known as the best 10-pound-plus bass water.

WHERE TO LOOK

To find big bass on Toho, I'll look for something different in the form of cover, e.g., a variety of vegetation. I'll fish the edges of those variances, where grass adjoins rushes, for example. That's where the bigger bass will lie. Taller reeds that grow in the middle of grass fields may be difficult to reach, but drop a large worm in there and hang on.

Brown's Point toward the southwestern shore has always been a favorite of mine. The maidencane and bulrush beds jut out into the lake several hundred yards and some patches are usually frequented by bass. Largemouth lie in many of the interior beds most of the year and are in the shallower stuff during spawning season. In April, though, they'll move to the outer edges of the rushes. This popular hard-bottomed bass area offers maidencane with scattered patches of rushes growing in about five feet of water. Fish the outside edges of the grass and around the mouths of boat trails.

Grassy Island is a grass point which once was separated by open water. It is a good big bass area with a mixture of dense maidencane and rushes in three to seven feet of water. The east side of Big Grassy Island has grass edges in five feet of water and is productive in the summer months. The depths occur relatively close to the shoreline, which offers a defined weed edge. Casting the boat trail mouths here can be effective. The west side of Big Grassy Island offers good bassin' in the numerous patches of rushes. The hard bottom and good deep water access, make this area an excellent springtime spot.

The scattered maindencane grass patches in four to six feet of relatively clear water at the back of Goblits Cove can be productive in the summer months. If water is moving through the St. Cloud Canal from East Lake Tohopekaliga, the currents will also attract schooling bass to the mouth of Goblits Cove. This action is normally found in the fall months.

Lanier Point along the west shoreline has trophy largemouth in its scattered rushes and dense maidencane in four to five feet of water. Watch for schooling activity around the grass and in the

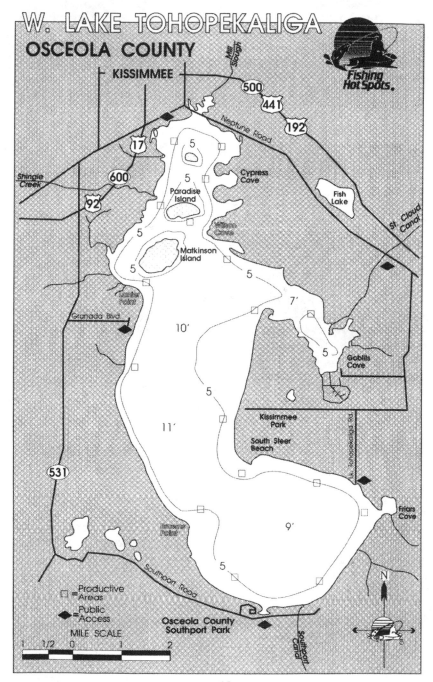

W. LAKE TOHOPEKALIGA
OSCEOLA COUNTY

KISSIMMEE

Mill Slough

500
441
192

Neptune Road

17

5

5

Cypress Cove

Shingle Creek

600

Paradise Island

Fish Lake

92

5

Wilson Cove

St. Cloud Canal

5

Matkinson Island

5

7'

Lanier Point

Granada Blvd

10'

5

Goblits Cove

5

5

Kissimmee Park

11'

South Steer Beach

Tohopekaliga Rd

531

9'

Friars Cove

Brownie Point

5

Southport Road

☐ = Productive Areas

◆ = Public Access

MILE SCALE

Osceola County Southport Park

Southport Canal

N

1 1/2 0 1 2

13

open water where mussel beds may be located. The grass patches around Paradise Island are also productive habitat for big bass.

Friar's Cove in the southeast corner of Toho is most productive during the spring months when the bass are bedding. Fish the maidencane edges on both sides of the mouth of the cove. During the summer months when rain is frequent, water flows from a tributary creek in the cove and provides good bass fishing. To the west, though, the grass around Whaley Landing is usually productive year around. The water depth along the outside edges of the maidencane and lily pads is five to six feet.

Directly across on the south shore near the Southport Canal are productive weed beds. Just east of Southport Canal exit, the thick maidencane grass in five feet of water is productive. The area of heavy maidencane just north of the Southport Park also offers excellent flippin' habitat. During January, February and March, the shallower stretches are where the bass are.

SIZING UP THE VEGETATION

Toho bass can usually be patterned according to irregular features of the vegetation, such as points, pockets, heavy clumps and matted reeds. I've found that the very best spot, however, is usually its transition to another type of vegetation. Deeper stretch of reeds abutting a submergent plant community will usually hold the larger bass.

Look for something different in the form of cover, and fish the edges of those variances. That's where the bigger bass lie. Taller reeds that grow in the middle of grass fields may be difficult to reach, but they are often productive. Largemouth lie in many of the interior patches of rushes most of the year and are in the shallower stuff during spawning season.

Vegetation communities sometimes look similar, but to catch bass consistently on Toho, look for those combinations. Another good example would be where pickerelweed or maidencane and hydrilla are intermingled. Toho bass prefer different types of aquatic plants at different times of the year, and even at different times of the day. They may be feeding along a grass bed in front of a reed line early in the morning and then move back inside the maidencane to the edge of rushes during the day.

The bass are generally tighter to the weed transitions when skies are brighter. Fish the darker areas along the plant variances first. Hydrilla beds against emergent grass is a good transition;

14

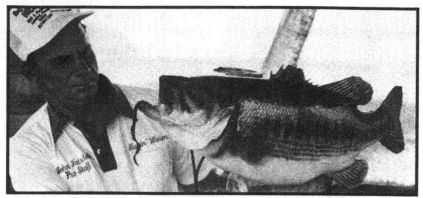

John Faircloth of Kissimmee caught the lake record "Toho" bass from Shingle Creek. It weighed 17 3/4 pounds.

likewise, pickerelweed and spikerush are also great combinations of cover. Such places are usually easy to fish effectively. Bass like the edges, and those weeds with a very definite edge against shorter vegetation are a magnet to largemouth.

Not all bass are in the heavy weed cover. One day a friend and I stumbled on a mussel bed in open water within sight of the Kissimmee city landing. Clusters of mussels get together and may cover several hundred square feet of bottom on Lake Tohopekaliga. Such an occurrence happens without a depth change. We caught (and released) a limit each from an anchored spot. Bass hold on such places because baitfish are attracted to the beds. Finding the beds, though, are difficult. I tried to find my way back to the one mentioned a month later and couldn't seem to relocate it.

TACTICS, LURES & BAIT

If an angler is lucky enough to see bass schooling over a bottom comprised of mussel beds, he should anchor and toss artificial lures. A crankbait is a great lure over such a bottom, and, in fact, more than one crankbaiter has retrieved a shell-fouled lure to discovery the mussels. The bed with big concentration of bass may be as little as 30 square feet.

Vibrating plugs, such as Rat-L-Traps, are effective when fished in the boat lanes and around the weedlines. Slender minnow plugs twitched in and around pockets in the maidencaine and buzz baits sputtered over short, sparse grass early and late in the day also fool many Toho bass. Scented plastic worms are productive in open waters and when flipped into the rushes.

I prefer to toss artificial lures on Toho, and plastic worms are usually very effective for me in the rushes and cattails. When the bass are spooky, stay back and pitch a Berkley Power Worm into the cover. Working it vertically along the deep edges can be very effective. Shake the bait, trying not to move it from that spot.

Most of my bigger fish (and those of others) have been taken on a Texas-rigged worm fished either by flipping or by casting. Drop the mouthful of plastic beside the tallest stand of reeds available. The clump doesn't have to span 1/2 acre, just 10 or 12 stalks is enough to hide a lunker. Ones with a cluster of white snail eggs are ideal. Bass often bump such stalks trying to dislodge the eggs so that they can feed on them.

Weedless spoons are usually productive in the shallower acres of maidencane grass and rushes during March and April. The big bladed spinnerbaits are also worth a try on the deeper edges of the weedline. So are topwater lures like Luhr-Jensen's Jerkin' Sam.

Several of my big Toho bass have been taken with huge native shiners as the bait. I have fished large native shiners a variety of ways in and around the boat lanes that cross the fields of grass. Each method has yielded some huge largemouth. Eight-inch shiners are hooked (generally for still, bobber fishing) through the dorsal fin with a 5/0 Brute hook. I'll hook them through the lips when trolling or drifting.

When drifting or trolling, the shiners are positioned five feet under a cork or free-lined. A wire weedguard is sometimes advantageous if the habitat is extremely dense. When fishing a boat lane or pocket in the vegetation, the baits are cast underhand to softly land near the cover. The rigged shiner is allowed to freely roam the area, towing a small, cork bobber. Trolling can be employed via the electric motor to pull the bait around the thick cover.

A nervous shiner may swim several feet away to avoid a fatal confrontation with a lunker bass. The observant angler should place that bait right back in the same area it was spooked from, for maximum action. Likeliness of a strong surge on the free-lined shiner should be increased. There is nothing more exciting than a bass breaking the white-capped surface about 40 yards from the boat and then jumping toward the sky, trying to free herself of the weedless lip jewelry.

Change bait often, just as soon as the shiner tires or is mouthed by a largemouth. Lively bait is essential to pull fish from the depths. Line testing 25 to 40 pounds and 6 1/2 to 7-foot rods with quality level-wind reels are what I use when shiner fishing. You'll need it when after the lunkers.

LAKE DETAILS

Being the sixth largest natural lake in the state, with a maximum depth of only 15 feet (a few deeper holes exist) and full of grass in three to seven foot depths, Toho has the area and habitat to grow giants. Lake Tohopekaliga is part of the Kissimmee Chain of Lakes and is accessible from Lakes Cypress, Hatchineha and Kissimmee, all to the south, via the Southport Canal (Kissimmee River) and S-61 Lock. The lake contains 22,700 surface acres and is approximately 11 miles long and 2 1/2 miles wide. While it has deep water, the average depth is only around five feet.

On the north end of the lake, Shingle Creek (the lake's headwaters) and the St. Cloud or "C-31" canal both run into the lake. Water levels currently are maintained by the U.S. Army Corps of Engineers lock and dam at the south end of the lake. In 1971, this lake was the first in the state to undergo an experimental drawdown to improve aquatic habitat and the fisheries. It was extremely successful and resulted in a tremendous fish production increase. Additional drawdowns every six to eight years has maintained a quality bass fishery.

Toho offers expansive fishing opportunities around its 33 miles of shoreline and 100 miles of interior weedline. Four islands, Makinson, Paradise, Grassy and Big Grassy, protrude through the tannic-stained waters. The heaviest growth of vegetation is on the northern half and the western perimeter of the lake. Brown's Point and the islands all have abundant grasses, as do shoreline areas as well.

The bottom is a mixture of sand and muck in the vegetated areas where dredging and restoration have not occurred, but the key to productive open water fishing lies in finding one of the mussel bed communities. There are also five fish attractors in place on the lake. The Game and Freshwater Fish Commission attractors cover an area of approximately 100 feet by 100 feet and are located in open water. They are marked by floating buoys painted white, black and orange.

The Florida Turnpike toll road and U.S. 441 and 192 all pass within a few miles of the lake, so it's easy to get there.

LAUNCH/GUIDE/NAVIGATION DETAILS

The lake basically runs north and south, and high winds on the lake can make for a rough day. The coves offer little protection from the white caps that churn up the shallow waters. Although the lake is part of the Kissimmee Chain and connects to East Lake Tohopekaliga via a canal, it is not accessible to boaters. You'll have to boat through the Southport Lock leading to Cypress Lake to escape the winds.

There are numerous launch facilities on the lake. The two most popular ramp areas are the Kissimmee Lakefront Park in downtown Kissimmee and the Southport Park facility on the southwest end of the lake.

The Kissimmee Lakefront Park on the north end of the lake is located a couple of blocks east off Highway 17-92 on North Lakeshore Boulevard. The nice park has a 6 lane ramp fishing pier, breakwater and marina docks. Osceola County's Southport Park lies off Highway 531 on Southport Road near Toho's Lock and Spillway. The park offers complete facilities including fee camping.

Another small ramp lies on the west side of the lake off Highway 531 on Granada Boulevard, and on the southeast side of Toho south of the town of St. Cloud is Whaley Landing. To reach the latter, you'll need to drive south off Highway 441 on Kissimmee Park Road to Lake Tohopekaliga Road and the public ramp. A little known ramp in excellent shape lies on the C-31 canal in the town of St. Cloud; Partin Triangle Park is south off Highway 441 and east of Kissimmee Park Road on Neptune Road.

Several fish camps and marinas also exist on the lake. In Kissimmee, there's Big Toho Marina, and a couple of others lie on the eastern shore, one off Pine Island Road toward the north end of Toho and the other off Highway 525 further south. Lying only 10 minutes from Disney World and a bit further from Orlando, most of the public facilities can get busy on the weekends.

For guide service on Toho, you can contact Dave Hoy, Professional Bass Guide Service, P.O. Box 91663, Lakeland, FL 33804-1663, phone (813)533-3865 or Capt. Shawn Foster's Fishing Guide Service, 105 La Riviere Rd., Cocoa Beach, FL 32931, phone (407)784-2610.

2

EAST TOHO'S BASS TRAILS

TOWING A BOAT behind me as I waded a perimeter boat "trail" off the shallow, marshy lake near St. Cloud was an interesting experience. The water clarity on East Lake Tohopekaliga was about five feet, but my wading was masked by profuse vegetation. The trail was loaded with points, pockets and a tremendously irregular edge to the bulrush and alligator weedline.

I had used the boat to reach the shallows on the far shore, and then took to the water for some "wet" angling. I towed my giant "floating tackle box" behind. By fishing from the wet side, I was able to keep tabs on water temperature variances. Most of the better areas had either an obvious thermal difference or an elevation change of only a foot or so. The temperature difference was easy to detect through my blue jeans and tennis shoes that day,

East Lake Tohopekaliga offers excellent clear water angling behind or in front of its perimeter weed line.

Even in highly vegetated waters such as "East Lake," as it is commonly called, bass react to variations in temperature, structure, pH and oxygen values. The wader can often find the structure and thermal variance without electronic equipment. The change in structure on that small lake was from pickerel grass to bulrushes, and the bass seemed also to concentrate at those spots.

The terrain and emergent vegetation was rugged when I slid into the relatively clear water that morning. Wading through mats and clumps of submerged and emergent vegetation can be difficult. But on my third cast, I was reminded why I was out there.

A four pound largemouth sucked in my spinnerbait and tried to make its way back into the heavy cover. I pressured her out of two clumps of weeds before I had her coming my way. The battle continued, as I stumbled into waist-deep water. The fight was more on my terms then. I pulled the bully bass from the weed entanglements and finally got her close enough to grab her jaw.

I unhooked her I watched her swim off slowly, obviously tired from that encounter. I continued my wading again and cast to the pockets and weed variations. The chartreuse bait attracted a second strike ten feet away from the same productive spot. Seven fish later I crawled into my boat and attempted to dry off a bit. It was time to leave.

East Lake's bass were not hard to find that day, but I didn't just jump into the water. I "analyzed" the body of water. The lake's shoreline was too marshy and shallow in one area and too deep with very little cover on another. The fertility of the soil, as denoted by the vegetation, and the moderate (wadeable) depth of the water in the area I chose to fish, were the reasons for its productivity.

The littoral area of the lake lends itself to wade fishing. The gradual slope of the hard sand shoreline and the variety of vegetation in waters less than 6 feet deep allows wading anglers to walk for miles and carefully work many spots. Boat lanes through the vegetation and stretches of open water between the bulrush perimeter adjacent the open water and the near shore grass beds are productive areas to cast.

The lake at the headwaters of the Kissimmee Chain is located on the edge of the town of St. Cloud, north of Highway 441/192. East Lake has a perimeter of bulrush, cattails, maidencane and torpedograss which provide excellent habitat for bass. Bulrush is found all around the shallow shoreline areas, and both maidencane and torpedograss are often found between the shore and the tall bulrushes.

Currently, the submergent varieties of vegetation include hydrilla, bladderwort, cabomba and elodea, which are found on the open water side of the perimeter bulrush line. Fells Cove has numerous beds of lily pads on its perimeter, and the two small ponds in Boggy Creek are covered with lily pads. The waters are very clear, as Florida lakes go, and water quality remains very good. Forage production, however, is minimal due to low basic fertility. In fact, East Lake nutrient levels are the lowest of all lakes in the Kissimmee Chain.

The Osceola County lake still produces excellent numbers of "harvestable" largemouth bass. Based on recent creel surveys by

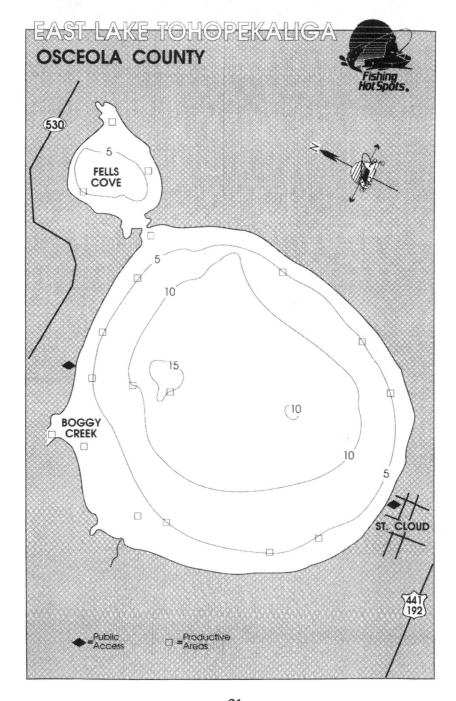

EAST LAKE TOHOPEKALIGA
OSCEOLA COUNTY

Fishing
Hot Spots.

530

5
FELLS
COVE

5

10

15

10

10

BOGGY
CREEK

10

5

ST. CLOUD

441
192

◆ =Public
    Access

□ =Productive
    Areas

the Game and Fresh Water Fish Commission, East Lake is one of the top-rated largemouth bass fishing waters in the state. Numerous bass between 10 and 14 pounds are taken from the lake each year, and every few years, a 15 or 16 pounder is caught.

THE WET SPOT

You generally won't catch the giants when wading the back alleys, but you'll have fun! The 'slowness afoot' involved in wade fishing such areas is an advantage in terms of productivity. Wading doesn't allow an angler to cover a lot of ground fast, but it forces him to fish more thoroughly than would the average boat angler. When the lure is presented repeatedly or closer to a bass, usually the chances are better for a strike.

An equally "wet" and productive way of catching East Lake bass allows an angler to access the deeper water off the bulrushes. Tubing is ideal, because you can climb into an inner tube and flip weighted worms into the tight cover without disturbing the habitat. The float tuber, or belly boater, as he's sometimes called, can slowly crawl a plastic worm with the patience and stealth needed to attract even inactive fish.

Waders often unsuspectingly step into small depressions and tubers don't. Even at six feet, two inches, I cast a much lower profile while settled into a tube than I do in my bass boat. That allows me to get closer to the fish-holding habitat, have better lure control and more leverage after the strike.

The belly boat consists of an inner tube which is partially lined with a cloth material. The commercially-made covering and seat is usually made of nylon which is rot and mildew resistant. Jeans and tennis shoes can be worn, but for more comfort, try chest high waders, either stocking foot or boot foot. They'll protect your legs from underwater obstructions.

Swim fins easily propel the craft when you are in water over waist deep. That is the most essential piece of equipment other than the tube and cloth seat. I found that out 30 years ago, when I first put together a float tube. I used tennis shoes to propel the crude craft constructed from an old patched up truck tire inner tube and denim seat. I quickly got myself a pair of fins.

Learning how to control the craft with swim fins was relatively easy. It took a few minutes, but once I learned how to kick upward to thrust myself backward and scissor-kick to turn the rig, I no longer had problems. To the first time tuber, the rig may feel awkward, but the feeling will pass if it's well constructed.

The advantage of a belly boater over a conventional boater is that he can "launch" just about anywhere around East Lake. This lake, with its 30-foot strip of eight-foot high rushes surrounding the open water, offers little weed-free opportunity for a wader. The water is six feet deep at the weed edge, so without the benefit of a tube, a deep-water angler needs a boat.

Due to its clear water, East Lake is also renown as a great night-time lunker bass lake. While the clear water is sometimes tough to fish during the high sun times, it is ideal for working after dark. Due to the lake's round shape, with ample development and lights, it is impossible to get lost here, even on a moonless night.

TACTICS, LURES & BAIT

Summer months are ideal for chasing night-time trophies, and the dark masks the need for light tackle. Lines of 20 or even 30 pound test can be employed when big bass are more prone to making mistakes. Heavy line will stretch less and can be safely used to pull a lure loose when hung up in the lake's thick perimeter vegetation. After dark, you'll want to keep your tackle to a minimum. Pre-rig several outfits with a variety of lures to minimize changes. Use a net, and avoid directing light beams over the water.

Winter months are best for daylight lunker bass fishing. The most productive method in the cold water times is to fish the bulrush line with wild shiners. Drift the line of vegetation with a shiner about six feet behind a small float. If the wind is minimal, use the electric motor to slow-troll along the weedline around the lake's perimeter.

Low light times, such as early and late in the day, during overcast skies and after dark are usually considered the best fishing opportunities for larger size fish on the circular lake. The low light times are optimal for those anglers who wish to fish the gradual sloping shoreline with weedless baits, such as spinnerbaits, slug-type worms rigs, spoons and plastic topwater fare.

Spinnerbaits and weedless spoons are very effective in the dense vegetation, and a trailer hook can be added for maximum hookup potential. White and yellow are good colors for the leadhead and skirt while silver blades are normally most productive.

Plastic worms are among the most productive lures to use on largemouth throughout the lake. Toss light-colored worms rigged Texas-style or Carolina-style to the deep bulrush perimeter or to the shell beds found in deeper water. Blue, red shad and pumpkinseed are good color choices. The worms dragged slowly down the slopes of deep dredge holes also work well.

Floating minnow plugs, topwater plugs, and vibrating plugs in silver with black back, silver with blue back, or gold with black back are also productive. Fish these around the vegetated areas on the perimeter and along canals and boat trails. Use the vibrating plugs and crankbaits in the deeper holes off the bulrush line and around the submerged hydrilla and elodea for larger bass.

Dark, weedless lures are best for fishing under the moon, because they cast a darker "shadow". The advantages of a single-hook lure versus the dual trebles of a large topwater are obvious. Curly tail plastic lizards and large plastic worm rigs that resemble snakes and other creatures of the night are effective. Blade baits with their thumping spinner action and surface plugs giving off steady rhythm during the retrieve can both result in jolting strikes.

WHERE TO LOOK

As the sun moves higher, bass in the clear waters move tighter to the deeper vegetation. After dark they roam the shallows, particularly along the western and northern banks. The Commission has placed six fish attractors in the lake that also draw bass. They cover an area of approximately 100 x 100 feet and are marked by floating buoys.

To find the lake's deepest holes (some are 30 feet deep), a good sonar unit is important. Bass take up residence in them during the temperature extremes. On the east side of the lake, one of the most popular deep holes is located just off the Boy Scout Camp. The fish hold on the drop which falls from six feet on the edge of the hole to 16 feet at the bottom.

Several other holes lie in the middle of the lake. Southwest of the largest deep hole in the lake's center is another deep hole that drops to about 16 feet. Some schooling bass can be found around these holes in the summer months. Water temperatures are about three degrees cooler in the dredge holes and about 10 degrees cooler in the spring holes during the summer. The dredge holes in this area provide bass with excellent depth and hydrilla cover.

Between the Boy Scout Camp and Lake Runnymede are numerous productive areas of scattered bulrushes and grass. It is a prime wading area with three to four foot depths. The grass patches are productive year around and the boat cuts through and behind the densest cover yield bass in the spring and fall months. The Runnymede Canal with masses of hydrilla along the banks can

Low light levels are good big bass times for anglers on East Lake Tohopekaliga.

be productive. The open water hydrilla patches just off that shoreline, and the pockets and cuts through the vegetation offer success. The depth along the bulrush line in this area is about a foot deeper than elsewhere on the lake.

The grassy weedline between the St. Cloud boat basin and the St. Cloud Canal yields bass in the fall and spring. The canal has adequate depth all the way to the locks just beyond Highway 441. When water is moving through the locks, this canal can yield numerous bass. Fishing in the boat trails and cuts behind the bulrushes is often good in the spring and fall months.

On the west side of the lake, check out the mouths of any gully or small creek after a rain when there may be runoff. In this area, the open water pockets behind the weedline are very productive. Fish them from a boat or wade the area for maximum stealth and lure presentation control.

The mouth of Boggy Creek flows into East Lake at two different places, and both provide good bass fishing. The main channel has additional water movement after rains and is usually more productive. The bass fishing in the spring and fall is productive on up Boggy Creek all the way to the bridge.

The two small open water ponds in Boggy Cove are offer lily pads and open holes which drop to 10 and 14 feet deep. The first pond area in the creek is the largest and deepest. In low light times, early and late in the day or during showers, boat on through the first pond and into the second smaller pond for action.

On the north side of the lake, the two canals from the mouth on in for about 50 yards are often productive. A large mussel bed can be found about 300 yards off the two canals. One lies beside a fish attractor, so it is not difficult to find. The grass patches in this area are productive year around and the boat cuts through and behind the densest cover yield bass in the spring and fall months.

The Fells Cove area has some excellent largemouth areas. On the north shore, lily pads and bulrushes in 4 to 6 feet of water yield bass in the cooler months. The southeast side is productive in the spring or summer months, as is the Fells Cove cut to the Lake Ajay canal. The mouth of that canal is particularly productive or schooling bass any time water is flowing after spring or summer rains. From the Fells Cove Canal mouth into the cut for 30 yards, bass are caught along the vegetation line.

Lake Details

The 13,550 acre East Lake Tohopekaliga averages about six feet deep along the bulrush perimeter and 10 in most of the open water areas. In some spots on the 15 square mile lake, depths of 16 feet can be found. Three waterways contribute to the 4 1/2-mile diameter lake: Boggy Creek on the northwest side, Lake Runnymede flowage on the southeast side, and waters from Lakes Hart and Mary Jane to the north via Lake Ajay and the lock east of Fells Cove. Underground springs help keep these waters clear.

A non-navigable lock at the outlet (on the St. Cloud Canal) off the southwest side of the lake helps maintain water levels. Water from East Lake flows downstream through Lake Tohopekaliga and the Kissimmee River system. The bottom on East Lake is mostly sand, but small rocks and shell beds, some covering about a mile and a half of bottom, exist in certain areas. During a 1990 drawdown, the state dredged built-up muck from 8 miles (of the 27 along the shoreline) on the west perimeter, generating new vegetation.

Launch access is rather limited at the time of writing. On the south side of the lake in the town of St. Cloud off Highway 441/192 is the popular East Lake Boat Basin. It's at the St. Cloud waterfront park on Lakeshore Drive. Most of the Orlando anglers use the East Lake Fish Camp ramps on the north side of the lake off Highway 530 (Boggy Creek Road). The popular resort complex offer several boat ramps, along with a complete service resort and marina. Guide service there is headed up by the renown Buck Johnson. His largest from the lake is one that weighed 14 3/4 pounds, and in 39 years, he has caught many, many 10 pounders. Contact East Lake Fish Camp, 3705 Big Bass Road, Kissimmee, FL 34744; phone (407)348-

3

OKEECHOBEE'S LARGEMOUTH FACTORY

I PULLED THE BAIT free of the stalk and watched it plummet quickly out of sight below the bush. The line twitched and then jumped to the side as a bass bolted from the cover. My hook set was late but adequate. Reeling furiously, I caught up with the hard charging bass and soon lipped it.

The two-pounder was freed of its worm hook and released. Two casts later, my partner took its twin as we circled the small stand of peppergrass and other vegetation that had grown up around a brushy area on Lake Okeechobee. Seven bass from the irregular 400 square foot weed clog was the reward for our dedication to the spot.

More largemouth swim in massive Lake Okeechobee than in any other lake in this country.

Our Texas-rigged worms were mostly gobbled up on the fall by the active spring bass. None of those largemouth or the other 10 we ferreted from another five similar spots were large - three and one-half pounds max. Seven inch plastic wigglers in moccasin, pumpkinseed and brown hues were productive for the smaller bass, but we weren't able to fool any giants on this day. With the lake so full of largemouth between one and four pounds, that's understandable, though.

Worming the "hayfields" of the huge Lake Okeechobee is usually a productive spring pattern for largemouth bass, and often, one of six to 10 pounds is the "anchor" to a significant "numbers" catch. Although bass in the lake seldom exceed 12 pounds, there are millions inhabiting the watery "Bass Factory" in southern Florida. Only the sheer size of the "Big O", as it is called by many, prevents it from becoming too crowded with bass boats.

Pollution problems originating from agricultural practices and watershed development have been a major concern to the lake's fishery biologists for many years. Excessive nutrients discharged into this system stimulated a massive bloom of blue-green algae during 1986 and resulted in low oxygen conditions and widely publicized fish kills. Fortunately, the bass fishery was relatively unaffected, but the need to monitor and prevent potentially damaging problems is more critical than ever, according to the Game and Fresh Water Fish Commission.

In 1981, the most severe drought on record lowered the lake and concentrated the bass population into deeper areas away from the shoreline. Water had receded several miles from the normal shoreline, leaving much of the vegetated lake bottom baking in the sun. Rains finally came and the lake started to refill. Then, vegetation blossomed and the low pH rose again to optimal levels. A severe drought in 1990 also lowered the lake and many areas of the lake were dry. The lake slowly started to refill, and minnow populations exploded. With the new water levels have come improved access and better bass fishing.

Navigation at normal water levels is generally hazard free. At low water conditions, that's another story. Many lower units are damaged on submerged rocky areas. Also, because it is shallow, Okeechobee can "blow up" in a hurry. White caps can cause concern for those having to run in such conditions. Hundreds of boat trails cris-crossing vegetated areas offer an escape from wind-whipped open water when caught in a sudden thunderstorm.

The bass-laden waters of Okeechobee are surrounded by dikes and have holes cut in them so that the water movement will not be inhibited. The farmland is rich in nutrients, and the dense vegetation is extremely attractive to forage. Some areas of aquatic growth are so thick that they are impassable. As a result, weedless baits and topwater fare are the most efficient over most of the lake.

Not all of the bass are buried in the vegetation, however. I was recently on the south Florida lake at daybreak searching for early schooling largemouth bass. After an hour's plugging of the sawgrass my livewell was still dry. Had two catfishermen not run their net nearby, the action might not have picked up.

I watched as a wooden, commercial rig pulled into the grassy cove. The men threw out a grappling anchor to snag the heavy rope that their net was tied with and soon pulled up a wire net with several fish flopping within. The catfishermen extracted the selected prey and dumped the remaining fish and other marine life

The hayfields of Okeechobee yield plenty of largemouth when water levels are up.

overboard. They rebaited their net and tossed it into the depths, moving on down the cove toward the next net set.

Quickly, I moved to the newly chummed area via the high-speed trolling motor. A 3 1/2 pound largemouth choked on my tail spinner lure and hit the cove's surface. I pulled him over the gunwale after his third leap skyward. A second quick cast resulted in another strike. I soon landed a twin of the first and both were released to grow up.

I continued to work the area where the net had been baited and where the majority of its contents had been dispersed in the water. My catch over the following hour was seven largemouth schoolers which averaged a solid three pounds each. The fish never did get active on the surface, but crank baits and tail spinners accounted for some exciting early action on open water just off the weedline.

A pH meter can help you locate bass anywhere on the lake, according to guide Walt Reynolds. Largemouth prefer a 7.4 to 7.9 range, but if no waters offer those readings, then fish the areas with pH values closest to the 'optimal' reading. In the more open water, schools of bass and/or their forage can be spotted on a graph, once the optimal area has been determined from the pH levels.

Most of the lake's bottom away from the vegetation is flat and structureless, but there are several areas where channels have been dredged for navigation purposes. You can check for them around the post-mounted markers with sonar. Other rocky reefs and shoals exist well offshore. Pay particular attention to the areas where the secondary canals enter the big lake.

Cuts, Canals & Catches

When the winds blow on the big lake, much of the fishing moves to sheltered waters, but the action doesn't stop. Canals, cuts and boat trails through the dikes, islands and dense jungle-like vegetation are productive to many. Hundreds of miles of the man-made waterways lie around the perimeter of the big lake.

The 100-yard wide Rim Canal with stands of tall trees protects anglers from winds and offers excellent fishing. The canal around the entire lake was the product of a massive 1930's flood control project. The 12-mile long canal on the northeast shore provides great bassin', as does the northwest section. Both have an irregular shoreline, and the canal portion paralleling the north shoreline also provides access to man-made feeder canals. The feeder canals there have boat docks and seawalls that concentrate bass.

The rim canal from Moore Haven to Belle Glade has primarily shoreline cover and heavy boat traffic during the weekends. When it was dug, irregular bottom was created, and as a result, some small ditches and depressions on the bottom can be viewed with a sonar unit. Fish the canal ledges which occur about 15 feet off the bank for bass action. Many of the secondary canals that link with the Rim Canal are 16 feet deep under normal water conditions. Uncle Joe's Cut (Mayaca Cut), Harney Pond Canal, Indian Prairie Canal and Taylor Creek are all productive bass spots.

Largemouth are also found beneath the bridges that span the canals leading into the lake. The running water around locks on some canals offer depth and a fresh constant supply of food, such as minnows and grass shrimp. Watch for moving water and corresponding currents around cuts and canal entrances. The canal waters are usually fairly clear with abundant vegetation along the shoreline.

A twitched surface lure, like the Luhr-Jensen Jerkin' Sam, will often attract big bass from the canal cover edges. The wooden topwater plug with spinner aft is productive for largemouth around any cover on this lake.

TACTICS, LURES & BAITS

There are often several patterns that are effective on the largemouth in this lake. Here's my approach: In the cold weather, I would fish the dense vegetation near the deepest water. During spring, I'd fish the open pockets in the sparser vegetation. Shiners work well in cool weather, so try 9-inch long baitfish with a 5/0 weedless hook for big bass action.

In the summer, lures like plastic worms and spoons are at their best. When the weather is hot, check out the grassline edges, the needlegrass and peppergrass clumps, "banana" bushes, "cornfield"

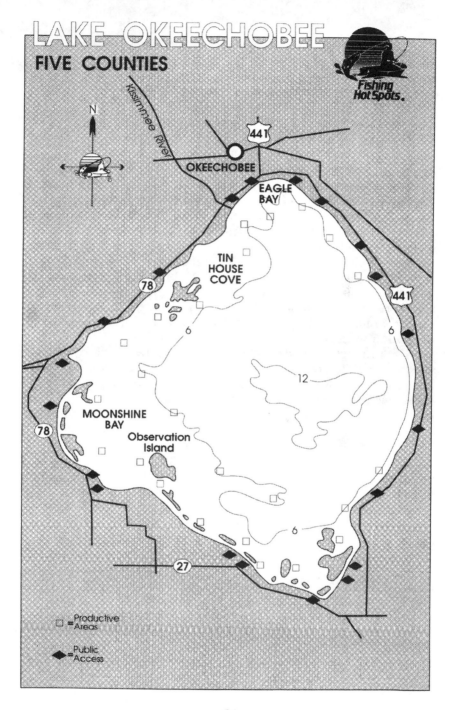

LAKE OKEECHOBEE

FIVE COUNTIES

Fishing
Hot Spots.

N

OKEECHOBEE

441

EAGLE
BAY

TIN
HOUSE
COVE

78

441

6

6

12

MOONSHINE
BAY

Observation
Island

78

6

27

☐ = Productive
       Areas

◆ = Public
      Access

31

areas and fence rows in the shallow water. Fish the points of grass and stay with any bass concentration you may come across. Try both the floating worm rig and the Texas rig in and around the weed cover. Toss a weighted worm around the needlegrass clumps and fence rows in the shallow, clear water.

Use a lightweight slip sinker, generally 1/8 oz or smaller, and a 3/0 or 4/0 hook. A 7-inch Berkley Power Worm in a red shad color with a curl tail seems to work well. On the Big O, you may want to move your worm a little faster than on others. Most of the bass will strike a worm as soon as it hits the bottom. Cast, let it sink, move it a few feet and then retrieve quickly for the next cast.

Also check out the grass lines with a long rod, line testing 20 pounds, and a 1/2 ounce weedless spoon with short plastic grub trailer. When bass are buried in Okeechobee's dense vegetation, they are often difficult to entice from their lair. A spoon will draw them out. The spoon is tied directly to the line without a swivel, and without a trailer hook. Just make sure that the hook is extremely sharp. The spoon is much easier to keep on top with the grub tail additive. The plastic grub has an action that doesn't deter the action of the spoon.

The productive spoon technique is best suited for heavy cover, such as hydrilla, grass, or heavy pad fields. Seldom will you miss many fish with this technique, because the bass hit it so aggressively. You need to keep the spoon moving very quickly, and as you reel it across the cover, you gently shake your wrist. That makes the spoon slap both the water and the cover.

The lure giving off a slapping sound moves quickly across the cover. This results, more often than not, in a reaction strike. When Okeechobee bass are tight to dense cover, they are usually not ruled by hunger. Surprisingly, it doesn't take much open water for a fish to come up and catch the disturbing source. The spoon should be hoppin' and just making a lot of commotion on top. Very seldom will you get hangups if the spoon is fished correctly.

Bass start schooling around mid-July on the big lake and keep on schooling until November. Check out the offshore reefs for schooling activity. Toss vibrating baits, crankbaits, surface plugs and tail-spinner lures at the topwater frenzy.

Move further back into the vegetation for maximum fall action. Try the noisy surface plugs early and late in the day around the open areas in the "hayfields." Rat-L-Traps fished along the edges of the grass also are effective. In the more colored or stained

Trolling the Rim Canal with crankbaits can be extremely productive.

water, throw spinnerbaits at the bass which can be numerous in two-foot depths. Try a buzzbait if after that trophy of a lifetime.

WHERE TO LOOK

On the west side of Okeechobee, the needlegrass flats and maidencane beds in the Monkey Box and Moonshine Bay areas are generally protected from the wind. The waters are normally clear and are prime spring areas. From Dyess Ditch to the southern point of Horse Island, known as "North Shore," there is a productive peppergrass flat that is well over 1/2 mile wide. Trophy bass hold in the outside edge of the grass on the west side of the bay. Sparse hydrilla patches mixed with maidencane, reeds and pads are primary spawning spots between December and March for bass.

The Monkey Box, named after an abandoned 30-foot tall wooden beacon tower constructed in the early 1920s, is the most important area on the west side of the lake in terms of bass fishery production. The current flows through this depression area which drops to about 7 feet, and bass tend to migrate in from Moonshine Bay and the entire Fisheating Bay area during the spring prior to spawning.

The spoil islands north of the Monkey Box area called the "Sand Piles" offer good bass fishing on the points. Several relief cuts there to allow water flowage from Harney Pond Canal into

Fisheating Bay. On the south side of the Monkey Box is the "Iron Stake Hole," a mixture of needle grass, lily pads, cattails, moss, ribbon grass and hydrilla. Emergent rock and the vegetation variety in this area provide a good spawning and holding area.

The 15-mile long Observation Shoal has reed and peppergrass over rocky bottom makes it one of the lake's largest spawning areas. The northern point of the shoal and the western shoreline area are both productive spring spots. Moonshine Hole's center is about two foot deeper than the area adjacent, and a natural current flow through the depression and the emergent aquatic vegetation attracts bass. Cochran's Pass with its bulrushes, reeds and scattered peppergrass near the mouth of Observation Island has excellent bass fishing. Current flow on all points from the wind tides make January through May the best months to try here.

Another excellent place in the Moonshine Bay area is the Cow Pasture, a 5,000-acre spawning ground. Bass will usually spawn throughout the entire area and then move into the nearby cover. Heavier concentrations of bass are found invariably in an area where there's just a little different or little thicker cover. Very thin "hay" covers the Cow Pasture, which actually used to be a cow pasture. It has crystal-clear water with pump trees growing out of excellent soil for spawning. That bottom is sand and shell.

The Moonshine Bay area is blessed with hundreds of acres of spike rush, maidencane, lily pads and needle grass, and the fish relate well to them. The shallow, weed-filled area will hold bass all spring. When bass move off the beds, the post spawners seem to move into nearby pads or other cover to recuperate. They're in a feeding mood, though, which is an excellent situation for the stretch of lily pads that runs approximately two miles in the bay.

To access that area by boat and be able to properly fish it, the lake has to be at the 14.8 or 15 foot elevation. At 16.5 feet, that area is just phenomenal for largemouth. Some of the best post-spawn areas are in two to three feet of water and have some beds of bonnets or dollar pads. The areas are slightly deeper than the spawning grounds, which attracts the post spawn bass.

Such places are difficult to locate, though, some having just one narrow trail going in and out. The access may be a boat width wide and about 400 yards long through a wall of cattails. Then, the tiny boat lane may break open into a depression one or two foot deeper than the remainder of the water. That's where you will find the bass. A couple of such spots are the Gator Hole, a depression 18 inches deeper than adjacent waters, and the Blue Hole, which

34

Worming the cuts and canals through the shallow grass flats of the "Big O" is usually very productive.

lies inside the rocky reef line. The water areas close to the open lake can get dirty when winds push across them.

Areas within and around Tin House Cove are very productive in the spring, as is the wide area on the backside of the emergent vegetation south of the cove toward Indian Prairie Canal. The area behind the cattails in the grassy flats offers good spring bassin'. Other good spots are the peppergrass beds from Indian Prairie Canal south to Horse Island and Warm Cove.

NORTH AND SOUTH SPOTS

Good bass spots on the north end of the lake are the flats stretching from the Henry Creek boat lock south to Chancey Bay, Nubbins Slough islands, rock piles, and boat trails, the rocky, weedy area north of King's Bar, Government Cut, and Eagle Bay. The latter is a prime largemouth area during the months of January through April when the lake is normally at its fullest. Bass hold on the peppergrass in the area.

The two-mile long Mayaca Cut and adjacent areas off Uncle Joe's Pass are good bass spots. Depth is about three foot deeper than surrounding water. On the south side of the channel, a series of spoil islands emerge close to the shoreline, and further into the lake, they generally exist just under the surface. The bulrushes, maidencane, peppergrass and other cover on the fringes of the islands and a good dropoff provide good fishing. The fishing is good along the full length of the channel, but the north side is generally more productive because of the current flow.

In the southwest corner of the lake, the sandy shell bottom of the West Wall is usually good. Scattered bulrushes and maidencane in about 4 feet of clear water (at normal levels) offer cover for largemouth and their forage. A rocky reef about 2 1/2 feet deep lies between the water tank's floating markers and Kreamer Island. This area is best when the water is low and clear.

Good spots on the lake's southern end include the heavily-vegetated Coot Bay area, the west and southeastern side of Ritta Island and South Bay. Fish the major grass flats, cattails, bulrushes and maidencane. The water here is fairly clear because it's sheltered from the east wind by the island. South Bay provides excellent fishing for open-water anglers. The mud bottom and numerous submergent grasses and mussel beds attract forage and bass.

The northern tip of Kreamer Island and Pelican Bay offer good action for spawning bass between January and February. In the summer, Airport Hole off the Palm Beach County Glades Airport is productive. The Pahokee Rocks area has little vegetation, but the boulders there provide good summertime action for big bass.

To find mussel beds on the big lake, toss a crankbait until it hangs up on the shell bed. Mussels usually migrate to the same area year after year. One bed is normally found off Horse Island. There is a two mile area of mussel beds throughout the area, and on the ends, there is pepper grass growing.

LAKE DETAILS

The 467,000-acre Lake Okeechobee is considered the "Mother of the Everglades." Although only averaging 10 feet in depth (with a maximum of 16 feet or so), it is the second largest lake entirely within one state. The Seminole Indian words "oki" (water) and "chubi" (big) correctly describe this lake. The lake basin encompasses 730 square miles at full pool and has a maximum length of 37 miles and a maximum width of 30 miles.

The headwaters of the lake are primarily through the Kissimmee Chain of Lakes. Waters leave the lake through a complex system of canals traversing the Everglades to the south and the channelized St. Lucie and Caloosahatchee Rivers to the east and west, respectively. The lake can be accessed from the east side, via the St. Lucie canal, from the west side, via the Caloosahatchee River canal, and from the north side, via the Kissimmee River.

The giant lake, with a drainage basin of more than 4,600 square miles, lies in Okeechobee, Martin, Palm Beach, Hendry and Glades

Counties. The lake is encircled by the Hoover Dike, a 38-foot high retaining levee. That levee and the Okeechobee Rim Canal lying just outside of it, allow for nearly total control of the lake elevation through a system of gates and pumps connecting six major flood control canals.

Elevations on the big lake are critical to navigation and fishing, and droughts and low water are not unfamiliar to locals around the lake. Levels below 13 feet are potentially dangerous, so use caution when leaving marked channels then. To navigate a long expanse to reach specific waters, a good map and local knowledge or assistance is advised. There are unmarked spoil islands as well as natural obstacles on the bottom. The lowest recorded level in 1990 was just above 10 feet, and nine feet is the lowest on record. The average elevation is around 14.5 feet above sea level.

The shores inside the dike are reed-lined, and thousands of acres of grass, called "hay fields," and hydrilla are scattered throughout the shallows. There are 151 miles of shoreline and numerous islands around the lake, including Kreamer, Torry, Ritta, Grass, Observation, Bird, Horse, Hog and Eagle Bay. Productive vegetation is also abundant. Drastic changes in types of vegetation on the big lake can occur from year to year.

The lake's extensive littoral zone and submergent vegetation communities along the western side extend from 1/2 mile to 9 miles wide. The weedline develops at approximately 5 feet. The east side of Okeechobee is essentially void of vegetation communities except on the southeast corner and the northeast section above Chancey Bay. While the western shore has the best-looking bass habitat and gets fished the most, fishing on the eastern shore can be very good. There is less shallow water in this area, and consequently, the fishing occurs deeper than on the western side.

RAMP/GUIDE DETAILS

Lake Okeechobee has some of the largest and best public launch ramp areas in the state. Most include a variety of facilities such as docks, camping, picnic tables, etc., and they are usually well-marked and easy to find. Boaters launching at some of the ramps must lock through the rim lock system to access the lake.

On the north side of the lake off Highway 78 just before it crosses the Kissimmee River is the popular Okee-Tantie Recreation Area. The future of this facility is in doubt at the time of this writing, but adjacent to it on the west side of Highway 78 is the expansive C. Scott Driver Jr. Recreational Area. Also relatively close is the Indian Prairie Canal Access Area.

Six access areas lie on the western shores of the lake off Highways 78 or 27. Just one mile east of the intersection of Highway 721 and 78 is the Bare Beach Access Area; just west of that intersection is the Harney Pond Canal Access Area; at the town of Lakeport is the Fisheating Creek Access Area; and further south is the Sportsman's Village Access Area. Off Highway 27 in the town of Moore Haven, just east of the Caloosahatchee River bridge, is the giant Moore Haven Recreation Area. Also in the town of Moore Haven off Highway C-720 on the west side of the Caloosahatchee River bridge is a small public ramp.

Four excellent ramp areas exist on the lake's southern end. Off Highway 27 in the town of Clewiston is the Clewiston Recreation Area; on the southernmost point off Highway 27 west of South Bay is the South Bay Access; in the town of Belle Glade off Highways 715 and 717 is the Belle Glade Recreation Area (on the southern tip of Torry Island); and on the southeast side off Highways 441 and 715 is the Pahokee State Recreation Area.

There are four good ramps along the northern part of the giant Big O. On the northeast side off Highway 441 is the Chancey Bay Access Area. Just east of the town of Okeechobee are two: the Nubbin Slough Access Area and the Taylor Creek Access Area. Off Highway 78 just west of the Highway 441 junction is the Lock 7 Recreation Area.

There are several rough ramps with limited parking on the lake. Two are located on the east side of the lake off Highway 441; one just north of its intersection with Highways 98 and 700 in the small village of Canal Point, and the other at the entrance of the St. Lucie Canal near the Port Mayaca Recreation Area. A third one which also accommodate 4-wheel drives and small lightweight craft best is on the north side of the lake off Highway 441 in front of the Henry Creek Lock and borrow canal.

Okeechobee guides include Larry Lazoen, 8 Prinville St., Port Charlotte, FL 33954, phone (813) 627-1704; Steve Daniel, P.O.Box 1972, Clewiston, FL 33440, phone (813) 983-3150; Chet Douthit, P.O. Box 87, Clewiston, FL 33440, phone (813) 983-3151; Jim Wells, Angler's Marina, 910 Okeechobee Blvd., Clewiston, FL 33440, phone (800) 673-9577, Bert Fischer, 249 Tropical Village, Clewiston, FL 33440, phone (813) 983-8902; Walt Reynolds, phone (813)983-8692 and Lance Glaser, 11440 Okeechobee Rd., #104, Royal Palm Beach, FL 33411, phone (407) 790-3869.

4

MARION'S SWAMP FISHERY

RAIN CLOUDS WERE skirting the area that afternoon, but we had remained dry. The weather overhead minimized our exposure to the sun during our fish catching activities. While the skies were threatening, the bass didn't mind. Friend Bob Lowe and I had experienced continuous action that morning. The Lake Marion bass had continued to feed and strike our lures without regard to the impending storms.

We had brought over two dozen bass to the boat and released them back into their weedy habitat. The action had demanded most of our attention, but suddenly, the lake quickly white capped with the onslaught of a 30-mile-per-hour gale. Willowy clouds darkened and a light sprinkle of rain fell.

Largemouth action in Lake Marion's profuse vegetation is an experience.

My partner was taking note of the increasing winds when he felt a strong tap through the deeply-bowed line. Bob leaned back hard to set the hook and met the resistance of a healthy fish. This bass was not like the others we had taken which ranged from one to about four pounds. The largemouth quickly moved off sideways, then leaped through the choppy surface waters landing on her broad side. Bob pressured the fish from the "jungle" and worked it toward the boat. Steady force worked the bass free of another weed entanglement about 10 feet away. The six-pounder again took to the air, trying to tail walk down the white caps.

The battle continued as the wind gusts blew our craft toward the shallow weed masses just off an island. Bob put more pressure on the bass and quickly grabbed her by the lower jaw and slung her over the gunwale. The rain pelted us as we released the bass and headed back across Lake Marion toward the Grenelefe Marina.

Lake Marion, not to be confused with another Florida water called Lake Marian which is located just east of Lake Kissimmee, is an excellent bass fishing lake near Haines City on the eastern edge of Polk County. While nearby behemoth lakes such as Kissimmee and Lake Tohopekaliga, grab much attention, this fishing opportunity can hold up to the best in the state. Much of the credit for the outstanding bass fishery should go to the influx of hydrilla there several years ago and to Illinois pondweed, another submergent plant better known as peppergrass.

GIANT LARGEMOUTH

The hydrilla and companion peppergrass fields in Lake Marion have reportedly given up largemouth to 18 pounds, and just two years ago, a 15 pounder was weighed in at one of the fish camps. During one October weekend, two anglers caught a one-day stringer of bass weighing 47 pounds. This catch included an 8 pound, 15 ounce specimen and an 8 pound, 2 ounce fish. At a local club tournament, 17 anglers once brought 250 pounds of bass to the weigh-in. Having fished Marion more than two dozen times, I know the lake normally produces plenty of seven-pound bass.

Guide friend Ronnie Wagers has fished the lake over 500 times and has often found the lake's big bass to be cooperative. On some trips, he and his party have caught and released over 100 bass. His largest bass was just over 9 pounds, but several customers have caught 12 pounders. The biggest bass that this guide ever personally hooked, however, may still be swimming in Marion.

Wagers and his guide party were on the southwest part of the lake when he hooked the giant bass. He had tossed a plastic worm on top of some lily pads, and as it rolled off, there was an explosion. At first, he decided that it was a small alligator, but once he got a glimpse, Wagers knew that he had hooked the biggest bass in his life. Unfortunately, the hook pulled free and the monster, which appeared to weigh 16 or 17 pounds, swam off.

While big fish are fairly common on Lake Marion, those two to four pounds make up the bulk of the catches. You can pretty much depend on catching a limit on Marion between February and April.

TACTICS, LURES & BAIT

One of the most productive patterns to use year around is a stick bait pattern. Try to keep the stick bait under the surface of the water about four to six inches, ripping it. This action creates an impulse reaction from the bass. The only problem in using a

Guide Ronnie Wagers has fished Lake Marion over 500 times and has often found the lake's big bass to be cooperative. This is an average-size fish for some of his better ventures.

minnow plug or stick bait is the vegetation which often causes hangups. The advantage of ripping the stick bait is that such a motion will tear it loose from the vegetation.

The stick bait pattern works because the hesitation gives the fish a chance to react to the lure. For those bass that can react fast, the Rat-L-Trap is very productive. The majority of Lake Marion anglers use either the Rat-L-Trap or a plastic worm. The latter in a red shad hue with glitter is productive over most of the lake.

The wind can be a factor on Lake Marion at times, especially in February and March, but anglers can also use the wind to help them catch fish. I've often drifted Lake Marion waters and caught bass from in front of the boat. Fish the lure in front of the boat or out about 30 degrees from the bow of the boat to avoid spooking the fish as you drift over the top of them.

The fishing is a little faster, but throwing into the wind is more productive. When the wind is really blowing, simply let it push the boat across the lake. High winds allow the boat to cover waters we wouldn't normally get to fish because of all the vegetation. Using a similar technique, one Grenelefe Marina guide and his clients caught and released over 50 bass during a 4 hour period.

Spinnerbaits, vibrating plugs, plastic worms and topwater baits all work well in the deeper holes around the lake. The bass may be congregated in such areas. Tossing a minnow plug should result in a response from a healthy supply of smaller fish. A Bill Lewis Rattle Stick, because of its weight, is one of the preferred baits; longer casts over the clear waters are attainable in any weather.

Dragging shiners behind the boat on Lake Marion is an effective pattern when the wind is blowing. Because of the profuse vegetation, using a cork with the bait positioned about two feet below is wise. Shiners are most productive December to May.

For maximum action, locate the deeper waters and fish the live bait around the mixtures of vegetation. Pulling the shiner along the outside edges of the peppergrass beds intertwined with clumps of hydrilla is productive. Areas around Bannon's Island, across from the Grenelefe Marina and across the lake from the county ramp are all prime areas in which to pull shiners.

WHERE TO LOOK

Some of the better areas to fish are offshore. A prime spot is located in the lake's center straight out from the public launching ramp. A ridge with five feet of water on top is the attraction. On each side of the ridge, roughly 200 yards wide, the depth drops to ten feet. Bass often can be found on or around the top of that ridge.

Lake Marion has numerous beds of hydrilla, peppergrass and eelgrass, and they are bass congregation points. One of the key factors to catching Marion largemouth is locating sparse combinations of vegetation. If you can find a combination in an area with open water adjacent to it, you'll also find bass.

Several dredge holes exist on the lake. Straight out from the county launch ramp is one that gets pounded constantly, yet it usually holds bass. Many anglers visiting Lake Marion for the first time will fish that 18-foot hole, the deepest water in the lake. Even with extreme fishing pressure, the hole attracts largemouth.

Another popular area is called Bannon's Island. On its northeast side, an east-west oriented trough with 10 to 12 feet of water extends almost to Shady Cove Marina. Working the outside edges of this hole is sometimes productive. When there's a lot of fishing pressure on this spot, however, the bass will move away.

Located just south of the Grenelefe Marina boat docks is a dredge hole with 8 to 10 feet of water. When the hydrilla isn't out of control, you can catch fish there. Boating straight out from the Grenelefe Marina docks in a southeastly direction will enable you to find another ridge which drops off to 12 feet of water. Such holes and drops are good places to check out.

CREEK DETAILS

The mouth of Marion Creek on the northwest corner of the lake is a very good bass fishing area. The main problem to anglers is the heavy vegetation. The open area around the creek's mouth is hemmed in by a cypress swamp bordering the lake.

When the creek is full, three to four feet of water exists, and there are some five foot deep holes dotting the creek bed. In low water, only small boats can access the majority of the creek. Canoes are ideally the way to explore the creek, which begins at a break in the sawgrass. The 10-mile stretch of Marion Creek between lakes Marion and Hatchineha, east of Haines City, is lush with magnolias, red maples and myrtles hovering over beds of eel grass, hydrilla and leaf litter in the meandering waters. Holly, Bay and sweet gum trees and wild flowers add colors to the landscape.

A few houses set back from the water for privacy and security, some docks, a one-lane wooden bridge and a modern bridge downstream of the other are about the only signs of civilization along the relatively clean-water creek. Local residents talk about widening and modernizing the one-lane wooden bridge, but they haven't done so for more than 10 years. A sand truck collapsed the structure in 1976, but it was repaired.

Creek waters beyond the wooden bridge are clear and shallow. Some activity along this stretch may be noticed during hunting season at an occasional primitive campsite, otherwise you're more likely to see a wild hog, turkey, deer or bobcat. Indian Mound Island separates the creek for about one mile.

LAKE DETAILS

The 3,000 acre Lake Marion lies just off state road 544. It is part of the 17,300-acre Marion Creek Basin in the state's fourth largest county, Polk. The lake's vegetation community is tremendous. According to a recent aquatic plant survey, Lake Marion has 600 acres of hydrilla and 240 acres of peppergrass growing from its fertile bottom. That's about 25 percent of the entire lake in habitat that encourages profuse growth of the entire food chain. While Marion is a relatively small body of water, only four other larger Florida lakes have more acreage of peppergrass.

In the lake's watershed are Marion Creek and Snell Creek. The latter drains waters from the town of Davenport to the northwest, and its waters are not as clean as those in Marion Creek, due to agricultural drainage. The waters clear up a few miles downstream of the source, however, thanks to wetlands filtration. Marion Creek empties into Lake Hatchineha and the Kissimmee River.

Speculation is that the lake was named after General Francis Marion, a Revolutionary War hero known as the "Swamp Fox."

The author finds a plastic Power Craw and slip sinker to be just what attracts a largemouth from the Lake Marion vegetation.

Considering the profuse vegetation in and around the lake and the topography of the creek's drainage basin, that's not inappropriate. Such abundant vegetation means that panfish and other forage are also numerous in Lake Marion.

Lake Marion has one free public landing and fee boat launch facilities at Shady Cove Resort off S.R. 544, Bannon's Island resort, St. Clair's Lake Marion Resort off S.R. 580 and Grenelefe's Marina off S.R. 546. Grenelefe Marina is part of the modern Grenelefe Resort and Conference Center, a 1,000-acre resort which includes three championship golf courses, a 20-court tennis complex, four swimming pools and 950 villa/suite accommodations nestled among huge oak trees. Information on bass fishing packages are available by calling toll free 1-800-237-9549.

The public launch ramp lies between Lake Hatchineha on the east and Haines City to the west, just off of S.R. 544. Take C.R. 542 to Jim Edwards Road, then turn north to the paved ramp. The public launch ramp lies on the southeast end of the lake about one mile past the entrance to the beautiful Grenelefe Resort Marina.

5

GRASS ISLANDS OF KISSIMMEE

FINDING A CONCENTRATION of bass embedded in heavy cover on Lake Kissimmee is not a rare event. That's where using a long rod and heavy line to gently drop a weedless offering into tiny openings within the grass is appropriate. "Flippin," as the popular method is known, is an ideal method for Kissimmee's bass.

With an underhand swing, you can cast into cover on this lake that's almost impossible to fish with conventional methods. You can maneuver the boat in heavy cover and sneak to within a few feet of bass that are hidden in the lake's dense habitat. When a largemouth grabs the bait, the stout rod will provide the leverage needed to hoist it out of the weeds.

The remote and undeveloped Lake Kissimmee with its islands, boat trails and weed jungles provides tremendous bassin'.

The typical Kissimmee bass makes its home in the thick aquatic undergrowth. Kissimmee bass usually escape pressure by moving further back into the thick of it, and in the heavy cover, they generally won't chase a bait far. Flippin' fish are not overly aggressive as would be feeders moving over a flat with sparse cover.

Lake Kissimmee's lily pads, bulrushes, reeds, maidencane, etc., all have the ability to become thick masses of seemingly impenetrable cover. Bass will burrow under such thick growth to find protection from their predators above, ample shade from the sun's rays and food. The most inaccessible places often yield the most largemouth because many anglers won't put forth the effort needed to fish such places. Flippin' is very efficient at presenting the lure to weed-bound largemouth, since very little time is required to replace the bait into another pocket.

I prefer to use rods that are seven feet long and have plenty of backbone. My choice are Berkley's Series One B50-7H Rods. They are designed to exert maximum leverage and power. They have a stout butt and backbone and a flexible tip to quickly set the hook. While any type reel can be used, most flippin' pros use the baitcasting variety. Positive drag and thumb control are the advantages to such equipment.

The line used in flippin' should be a premium quality, abrasion-resistant monofilament, 20 to 30 pound test. It should be low stretch and tough enough to survive the constant interaction with heavy weed growth. I use Trilene XT or Tri-Max monofilaments.

I've found that both plastic worms, rigged Texas-style, and jig and eels work well on Kissimmee. A heavy-duty 5/0 worm hook is what I prefer for hooking trophy bass in tight quarters. The best slip sinker is 1/2 ounce, but often a lighter (3/8 ounce) or heavier (3/4 ounce) weight may be required. The size will depend on the cover being penetrated. The sinker is pegged with a toothpick so that it won't wander away from the worm. A scented worm is ideal for flippin' Kissimmee's cover.

If the "jungle-type" cover appears impenetrable, this is prime habitat for the largemouth. Try the thickest cover first and then work the more sparse aquatic terrain. When two or three types of vegetation co-exist, try the denser variety initially, then work the area where they intersect. The flippin' technique is most successful in off-color waters, those tained naturally or by rain runoff. Bass are easier to approach in the murky surroundings.

Fish the shady side of any cover that you come across. That's where bass will try to hide. Likewise, they'll move further inside a weed mass during a pounding wind. They don't like to be jostled about by wave action. The taller and thicker the weed growth, the better. Thick clumps often grow in sandy soil and fairly deep water hundreds of yards off the shoreline. Values of pH are most often ideal in such areas.

NUMBERS AND TROPHIES

Lake Kissimmee is one of the top five largemouth bass areas in Florida, according to creel surveys. In an average Florida lake, the fishing success rate is .25 largemouth per hour. In Lake Kissimmee, that rate is usually over .40 bass per hour in the summer months. The lake has always been a trophy bass producer and reports of largemouth near 17 pounds occur every few years. Over the years,

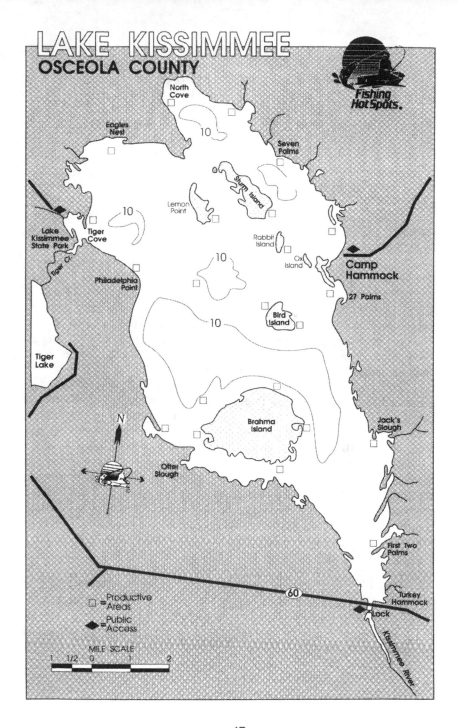

LAKE KISSIMMEE
OSCEOLA COUNTY

Fishing Hot Spots.

North Cove

10

Eagles Nest

Seven Palms

Slum Island

Lemon Point

10

Lake Kissimmee State Park

Tiger Cove

Rabbit Island

Ox Island

Camp Hammock

Tiger Ck.

Philadelphia Point

10

27 Palms

Tiger Lake

10

Bird Island

N

Brahma Island

Jack's Slough

Otter Slough

First Two Palms

60

Turkey Hammock

Lock

Kissimmee River

☐ = Productive Areas

◆ = Public Access

MILE SCALE
1   1/2   0   1   2

the lake has provided tens of thousands of 10 pound largemouth. Fishing pressure has almost doubled in the past 10 years, but the lake has been able to support the trophy bass attention.

One of the reasons for the continued productivity of Kissimmee is lake management. In 1977, the water level was lowered by 8.5 feet, exposing 45 percent of the lake bottom. Bottom sediments were consolidated and the vegetation communities were improved. The lake drawdown has proven to be a very successful management tool in limiting the effects of stabilized water levels and over-enrichment of several lakes in the Kissimmee Chain.

While Lake Kissimmee receives most the year-round attention, its two "sisters," Lake Hatchineha and Lake Cypress, often offer spring bassing that is difficult to top.

The 6,665 acre Lake Hatchineha has a standing bass crop of around 50 pounds per acre. Creel surveys by Commission biologists have shown that approximately 3,400 bass are harvested annually from the lake. Bass fishermen released about half that number also, which bodes well for conservation and the future of the fishery there. The voluntary release rate for bass under 12 inches runs about 96 percent, too. The state's new 14-inch minimum should promote continued conservation.

Hatchineha is perhaps the prettiest lake in the Kissimmee Chain with its cypress trees and variety of vegetation. Additionally, there are many points, inlets, small bays, pot holes and boat trails to add variety of scenery. Just four miles to the north is Cypress Lake, which ironically doesn't have many of its namesake trees.

Cypress, a flat 4,097 acre lake just north of Lake Hatchineha, is often overlooked by local bass anglers. Its popularity with out-of-state anglers, though, is significant. According to a recent spring survey, over 30 percent of all fishermen there were non-residents. The rushes and cattails on the perimeter of Cypress typically holds the concentrations of bass. Studies by Commission biologists there have shown that about one of every three bass caught are released alive.

Most of Cypress Lake is surrounded by wilderness, with some shorelife to be found on the east side around a small boat ramp. Just south of the ramp at Cypress Lake Road is Canoe Creek which can yield bass when the water is running through the water control structure. The mouth of Reedy Creek on the western shore offers good bassin' under the same conditions.

My favorite bank on Cypress is the northwest shoreline, just east of the canal. That's where I've caught several largemouth up

Lake Kissimmee bass are usually fat and strong fighters.

to 10 pounds. The reed edge is most irregular in this area, and the shallow shoreline is just slightly deeper.

Fishing the pockets and points in the emergent vegetation will pay off. My partner and I observed a big bass chasing a bluegill from one of the pockets, and we fished that area for about 20 minutes two different times trying to entice the fish. We left it for an hour a second time and returned to catch the nine pounder on the first cast back into the pocket!

Just north of the lake is the famous Southport Canal or C-35, which transports outflow from Lake Tohopekaliga four miles to Cypress. That's the location where a couple from Iowa caught 20 largemouth weighing over 151 pounds in 1977. In the late 70s, I caught about 30 pounds of bass along the canal in an hour's time to win a big bass tournament. The canal today offers variable bass fishing when the boat traffic is not too bad.

For more information on the "overlooked sisters" in the Kissimmee Chain, write Ed Moyer, Fishery Biologist at Game and Fresh Water Fish Commission in Kissimmee.

TACTICS, LURES & BAITS

Whether the seasonal pattern is any good or not depends on the weather. Most of the lake's guides prefer to fish in hot weather because they'll generally catch bigger fish. Topwater plugs and jerkbaits can be very productive under low light conditions. One with a spinner at the back may be most effective. During the spring and fall, light factors influence the bite less, so the pattern holds as long as the weather is fairly cool.

A plastic worm, Texas-rigged on 12 pound test line, is ideal for water that is clear and shallow. With such a rig, you may expect a dozen strikes or more from small Kissimmee largemouth. Always a productive lure on the lake, a weedless spoon can be effective. When the bass are very active, use a silver spoon with small worm trailer. On cloudy occasions, gold or chartreuse spoons seem to produce better.

Live shiners are also very productive on trophy largemouth. Shiner fishing experts suggest anchoring on vegetation or drifting the hydrilla-infested areas on Kissimmee. Areas with a two foot drop are most productive, if you can find them. A small cork bobber can be employed in and around thick cover. The bobber should be 1 3/4 to 2 inches in diameter and sized to allow the shiner to pull it under only when expending full energy.

The wind can be utilized to move the boat and shiner rigs over submerged grass flats. The drift method is productive when used along underwater ledges of hydrilla. An electric motor is generally necessary in tight areas where emergent cover is dense, in waters protected from the wind, along bulrush areas with an irregular pattern and during strong wind.

Line testing 20 to 25 pounds, seven foot rods and level wind baitcasting reels are often the chosen shiner tackle. The baitfish are normally fished one of two ways, either five feet under a cork, or they are free-lined from the drifting boat. Hooks ranging from 4/0 to 6/0 are sized according to the length of the shiner. Implant the steel hook through the shiner's lips for the wind-aided trolling.

The shiners are cast underhand to land softly and then watched. As the baits become excited, they will frantically struggle to get away. A nervous shiner may swim several feet away to avoid a fatal confrontation with a bass. The observant angler should allow the bait to remain in the same area that it was trolled over for maximum action. Move if you haven't seen any action within 20 or 30 minutes. Moving frequently is often required to find a concentration of bass on Lake Kissimmee.

Tight-line big shiners using conventional level-wind tackle with small split shot sinkers and a strong hook. When a concentration of largemouth is located, anchor both ends of the

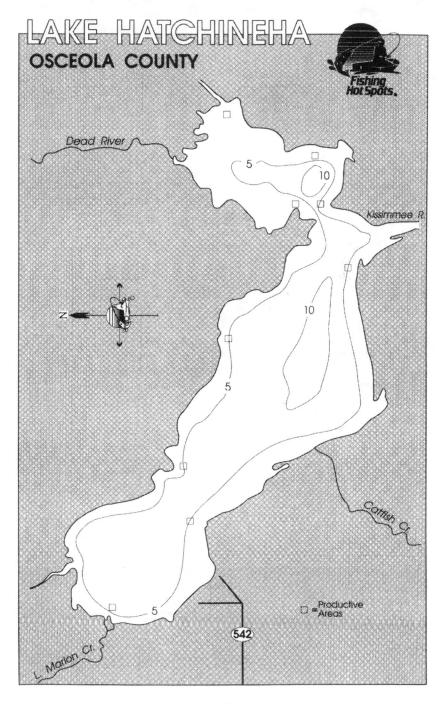

LAKE HATCHINEHA
OSCEOLA COUNTY

Fishing
Hot Spots.

Dead River

Kissimmee R.

5

10

10

5

Catfish Cr.

5

□ = Productive
Areas

542

L. Marion Cr.

N

51

boat securely and place three or four dorsal-hooked baitfish on the bottom in 6 to 10 feet of water, allowing it to freely roam the area along both emergent and submergent vegetation.

WHERE TO LOOK

Concentrations of largemouth are often predictable during the summer months on Lake Kissimmee. The maidencane and other types of scattered grass on the lake may be two miles from the shoreline in some places and near the shore elsewhere. Two areas that provide the most vegetation and bass are North Cove and Philadelphia Point. North Cove has both hydrilla and peppergrass that make it a productive bass area in the summer. In the fall, successful anglers will fish the outside vegetation edge. The Seven Palms area there offers abundant shallow lily pads that hold bass along their outside edges.

The outside edges of the maidencane, bulrush and other emergent vegetation, and the hydrilla pockets off Philadelphia Point, are magnets to bass, particularly in the springtime when water is high and the combinations of different vegetations are flourishing. Numerous boat trails criss-cross most parts of the weedy point, and they yield bass. Largemouth spawn in this area in two to four feet of water around the pads and reeds in the spring.

Nearby, is Grassy Island, a combination of maidencane, lily pads, hydrilla, peppergrass and other aquatic vegetation. The bass fishing on the mile long stretch of cover in water depths of three to seven feet is excellent from early spring to late summer. The area between Grassy Island and Lemon Point provides good bass fishing in the open water around the hydrilla patches. Pay particular attention to the isolated patches and holes in the hydrilla.

The northwest corner of the lake has recently been blessed with abundant hydrilla, making the area excellent for summer bass catches. This area also offers scattered vegetation consisting of hydrilla, peppergrass, lily pads, reeds and maidencane, plus pockets of open water. The area here is often protected from a north wind. Guides and other knowledgeable anglers select their location on Kissimmee depending on which way the wind is blowing.

Some other areas to avoid strong winds are around Brahma Island. On the southeast corner, fishing the hydrilla at the edges of the dropoffs along the cut is productive. The depth varies from two to eight feet and averages four to five feet off the main channel. The cut behind Brahma Island between Rocky Point and Otter

Slough is an excellent summer spot for largemouth bass. The fish congregate in the combination of pads and hydrilla. The western most point of Brahma Island offers a good dropoff and combination of peppergrass, pads and hydrilla.

The Highway 60 bridge on the south end of the lake is a good summertime area for those who can fish the deep water around the bridge pilings effectively. This area is excellent when the S-65 lock is open and water is moving out the Kissimmee River canal below. There is a series of canals between the Shady Oaks Fish Camp and the Highway 60 bridge that provide good springtime bass action. A dropoff near the river channel creates holes in the hydrilla and scattered peppergrass patches, and bass love the area.

The Twenty Seven Palms area is one of the lake's most popular bass spots. The outer grass lines are productive in the summer, and early in the spring, the one to four-foot shallows are one of the first places bass will move to spawn. The area will yield bass all year if you vary the depth of your fishing, going shallower as temperatures become cooler. Nearby Bird Island has good summertime bassin' in its hydrilla growth in four to six feet of water. At either location, move into the shallow vegetation early or late in the day. Boat trails over hard sand bottom provide adjacent areas for spawning during the spring, so check them out as well.

Rabbit Island and Ox Island offer good fishing in the cooler months. Try the west side of Rabbit Island for big post-spawn bass. Fish along the edges of the hydrilla and maidencane and in the open pockets within the vegetation. The east side is also productive, particularly along the inside vegetation transitions. The point of Ox Island is a good contact point for bass. Fish the outside edge of the scattered hydrilla which abuts water 10 feet deep.

The Polluted Water area, a name only, provides good spring and summer bass angling. Fish the mouth of the cove around the scattered hydrilla and peppergrass patches which are mixed in with maidencane and other grasses in five to six feet of water. Shallower depths in this area are also productive in the early spring when spawning fish are moving about the hard sand bottom.

On the east side of the lake are several excellent bass spots. The Jack's Slough area is productive in the late spring and summer months. The edges of vegetation are especially good after rainshowers when water is moving through Jackson Creek to the lake. The Three Oaks area offers scattered hydrilla patches in seven to nine feet of water, and bass are abundant. Fish the outside grassline when the hydrilla allows as early as possible in the year.

On the northwest side of the lake, the Tiger Cove area provides excellent bass fishing when water is moving through Tiger Creek. The water comes from Tiger Lake which offers some good bassin' as well. Try the point on the east shoreline about two thirds of the way down the lake from Tiger Creek. Also check out the southernmost shoreline vegetation and the northeastern shoreline plant communities on Tiger Lake. Nearby, another player on the Kissimmee Chain team is Lake Rosalie. Try the point on the lake's western shoreline and some of Rosalie's deep water holes for a good chance at the lake's largemouth. Both Tiger Lake and Lake Rosalie have productive fish attractors placed in them by the state.

Back on Lake Kissimmee, the mouth of the dredged Kissimmee River from Lake Hatchineha is an excellent largemouth bass area year around, especially when water is moving. There is schooling activity in the 20 foot deep waters, particularly during high boat traffic. The southeast side of Lemon Point is an excellent spot for trophy-size largemouth. Also check out the mouths of the boat trails that cross through waters from three to six feet deep.

During the hottest months, the locals sometimes focus on the Kissimmee River and canals and creeks feeding it. Bass can often be easier to pattern on the river during hotter periods; they will generally be holding on the reed patches, eel grass patches, and points. You can often catch a few fish off any docks you find.

In Lake Hatchineha, the grasslines in four to seven feet of water near the mouth of the Kissimmee River are excellent summertime spots. The scattered hydrilla and grass combinations in conjunction with a quick drop near shore to 10 or 12 feet, such as that found along the eastern side of the lake, is especially productive. Fish around the openings in the grass off the points and along the outside edges of the grasslines for summer bass.

The grass edges near Lake Marion Creek and London Creek on the northwest side of Hatchineha are productive early summer spots. The canals in Hatchineha Estates on the west side of the lake yield bass in the spring months, as does the mouth of Catfish Creek also on the west side. A couple of old fish attractors in open water can concentrate bass in the hotter and colder months too.

LAKE DETAILS

Lake Kissimmee, located about 60 miles south of Orlando and 20 miles east of Lake Wales, is the "anchor" to the Kissimmee Chain of Lakes. The chain also includes lakes Hatchineha, Cypress,

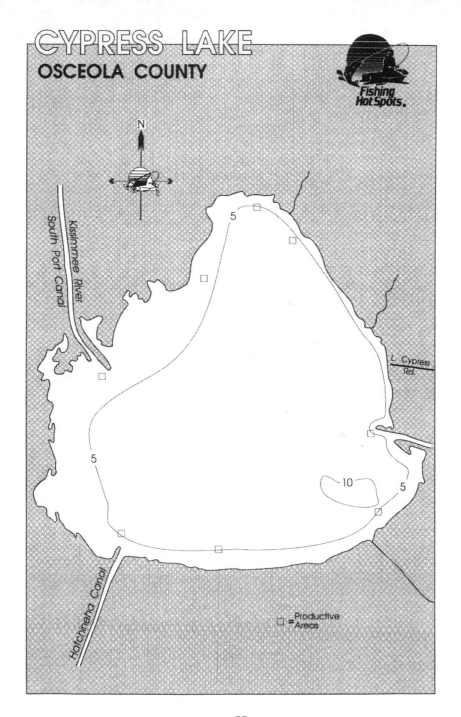

CYPRESS LAKE
OSCEOLA COUNTY

Fishing
Hot Spots.

N

Kissimmee River
South Port Canal

L. Cypress Rd.

5
5
10
5
5

Hatchineha Canal

□ = Productive Areas

Tohopekaliga and East Lake Tohopekaliga to the north. The Kissimmee River drains the upper basin into Lake Kissimmee and after leaving the lake, flows southward into Lake Okeechobee. All of those lakes on the Kissimmee River above, with the exception of East Tohopekaliga, can be reached via navigation locks.

The 44,000-acre Lake Kissimmee with 115 miles of shoreline is the most remote of the state's 10 largest highly-acclaimed bass waters. It averages about nine feet deep. The Upper Kissimmee Basin covers 200 square miles and includes 26 lakes with more than 110,000 surface acres. The lake is about 18 miles long and 6 miles wide with three inlets: Tiger Creek, Jackson Creek and the Kissimmee River. A dam and lock on the south end of the lake at the outflow of the Kissimmee River controls the water levels.

There are seven islands in Lake Kissimmee, all surrounded with dense vegetation. The heaviest growth of plants is on the north end of the lake in North Cove and west of Lemon Point. In all, there are about 15,000 acres of vegetation on the lake. Lake Kissimmee has abundant spatter-dock, fragrant water lily and American lotus. The pad communities are found along much of the perimeter shoreline areas and many of the shallow islands.

Pickerelweed, maidencane, torpedograss, cattail and arrowhead are scattered throughout the extensive littoral zone of the lake and provide excellent cover and spawning habitat. The primary submerged vegetation, hydrilla, and the prevalent floating type, water fern, both comprise over 3,000 acres on the lake. Changes in vegetation acreage and type can occur from year to year.

Only a few public boat launch sites are available on the undeveloped lake. The Kissimmee State Park on the west side of the lake off Camp Mack Road has an entrance fee, but the ramp/marina area is beautiful. The pristine 5,027-acre park also has canoe rentals, observation tower, marked nature trails, and great picnic facilities. On the south end of the lake off Highway 60 on the west side of the Kissimmee River bridge are two ramps: one above and one just below the S-65 Lock and Spillway. The Joe Overstreet Ramp is on the east side of the lake off Highway 523 and Joe Overstreet Road. Several fish camps also offer fee launching.

For Guide Service on Lake Kissimmee, contact Dave Hoy, Professional Bass Guide Service, P.O. Box 91663, Lakeland, FL 33804-1663, phone (813)533-3865; Barry Weaver, Bears Bass Guide Service, P.O. Box 4176, Lake Wales, FL 33859-4176, phone (813) 439-3769, and John McKnight, Jr., 3542 Creekmur Lane, Lakeland, FL 33813, phone (813) 646-5635.

6

KISSIMMEE DOES THE TWIST

DORMANT FOR ALMOST a quarter of a century, some of the Kissimmee River "oxbows" are once again living. This rebirth of sorts is sure to enhance the bass fishery and provide additional opportunities for all anglers along the rejuvenated river. Now in its early stages, the Kissimmee restoration should provide more than political excitement; it should have a positive impact on several hundred miles of waterway and the vast Lake Okeechobee.

The Kissimmee River has received its share of press over the years, but little has dealt with the bass fishing along the expansive waterway. Most has concerned the controversy around its channelization between Lake Kissimmee and Lake Okeechobee between 1963 and 1971. Pollution and environmental damage along the Kissimmee River, and in the huge "Big O" as a result, has garnered the headlines.

Putting the Kissimmee River back into its old channelswill double the bass fishing opportunities.

Described by many sportsmen as the "costliest mistake" the Army Corps of Engineers ever made, the river and government are again posed for some significant headlines. After ditching the river and dividing it into a series of five pools, each with its own water control structure, at a cost of $30 million over 10 years, the South Florida Water Management District plans on restoring most of it into its original winding channels.

The decade-long project costing over $350 million will meander the remote parts of the river once again. The project if it proceeds as now planned is the most extensive river restoration project ever undertaken anywhere. Completion of Phase 1 with continued funding, will take three to five years.

The demonstration work, in fact, is underway. Phase 1 of the Kissimmee River restoration demonstration project began in 1984 with the installation of three sheet-pile weirs in Pool B. Separation berms and culvert installation were completed in 1986. Baffle blocks at each of the locks to reduce erosion were installed by the Corps at that time. The structural aspects are designed to divert water back into historic oxbows and formerly existing marsh lands.

Fishing in the waterway can be excellent, or it can be slow, depending on your ability to solve some of the river's complexities. Knowing what the current is doing and not doing will aid the angler in selecting the best spots to work along an existing waterway with a variety of shoreline cover and some bottom structure variations.

Larry Lazoen is a guide friend familiar with the river and the Kissimmee River Restoration Project. I recently fished Pool B with Lazoen, who is familiar with all of the pools on the river. Most of my fishing experiences on the river have occurred in Pool A, between the first lock at the Highway 60 bridge just south of Lake Kissimmee and the second one about 10 1/2 miles south.

I have caught some nice strings of largemouth in Pool A over the years, despite the channelization. By fishing the points where the main flood control channel, called C-38, passed by the old river channel, I was able to catch several bass up to seven pounds. Overgrown canals off the old river channel also provided great bass fishing. On one weekend, a friend and I caught and released 40 largemouth in one canal. Anywhere else along the old river bed, though, has usually been void of bass, in my experiences.

Lazoen had fished Pool B, located about 14 miles east of Sebring, several times and was familiar with C-38. We all were surprised, however, on our first jaunt up a restored river bed. As we wound our way upstream through twisting overgrown shorelines, we passed underneath a red-tailed hawk. It remained on a leafless branch seemingly undisturbed by our presence and the sound of our outboard. We paused to take a picture, and the bird took to the sky with the sound of my camera's motordrive advancing the film.

Shortly afterwards, we began wetting our lines. It wasn't long before a feisty bass sucked in my plastic worm and darted toward the overgrown vegetation. The powerful fish, although on the short side of two pounds, headed into a weed thicket in three feet of water. Steady pressure led it out and to the boat.

The small canals off the Kissimmee River can provide interesting bass action.

The bass had a typical river shape, short and chunky. The coloration and shading is similar to those largemouth found in lakes, but the river bass are usually thicker than their leaner cousins. I released the fish and watched it swim back toward its home near the old river channel's overgrown shore.

CURRENT DETAILS

We figured that the current must be pushing 5 mph in the channels recently employed by water moving around the three new weirs. That's a healthy current, and in some areas, even the most powerful trolling motor won't make progress against the river. Get hung up, and you'll have to start the main engine, unless you are on one of the secondary channels that doesn't receive the full force of the river.

When you drop in a worm or slow bait, by the time you pick it up, it has washed downstream several yards. As a result, the old river channels with less current are more fishable. We found one that was off the main channel yet had some water movement, and considered that ideal. While not in the mainstream, those tributaries with some current flow will still be deeper. They'll be cleaner and provide better fishing too.

In the rainy season, the oxbows will have good current flow. When they are dropping the river and putting water into Lake Okeechobee, it will be flowing primarily in the main waterway. Runoff from rains will affect the ones that are primarily slack water most of the time.

Fish in a river are always repositioning themselves according to flow. In a relatively stable lake system, fish will take a position and stick with it for awhile - through a season. In the river, the bait and cover may change from day to day, and so do the bass. It's a little trickier. You can have a very good day, and then go out the following day and do the same thing in the same areas and not find them. They still may be there, but the fish could be repositioned on the cover or they may indeed have moved.

TACTICS, LURES & BAIT

Transitional periods like the pre-spawn time we were fishing can be tough. Bass may be moving and feeding some, but there can seldom be a strong "pattern" developed for catching them.

Fishing the river channel when the current is going one way and the wind is blowing another can pose problems. Unless you're in a gale, the boat will drift with the current, and you'll have to fish as fast as you can. You won't have many chances at a specific spot along the Kissimmee where flow exists, unless you boat upstream and drift by it again.

River bass will usually hit a plastic crayfish on the drop. One which can be flipped into any little hole in the floating vegetation is ideal. Pitchin' and flippin' into the heavy cover is most productive. The depths under the vegetation may range from one foot to 15 where it has grown right out over the river channel.

In the spring, bass may be on the first drop in waters less than 10 feet, while summer fish may be deeper on the second dropoff. Deep-running crankbaits and Texas-rigged worms or plastic crayfish are effective in depths of 10 to 20 feet.

The weirs themselves may hold some bass. Those banks just below them that have a high bank should block some of the current and provide bass a resting spot. The bass want to get out of the current flow so that they don't have to continuously fight it.

In late spring or early summer, crankbaits can be productive. Throw them at the mouths of the cuts and across each point you can find. Some of the Kissimmee waterway has islands whose perimeters can be fished. In shallow vegetated areas, toss a spinnerbait for maximum action.

In the summer, top water baits are also excellent along the river. Throw them early and late in the day along the edges of cover. Bass will be positioned on the edge of the cover during overcast conditions or low light levels and will come out for a properly presented lure. As the day progresses, it is often best to switch to jerk baits such as the minnow plugs and then onto hard or fast-moving baits. As the sun's rays become more intense, slow

The author finds big bass action along the old river channel that now contains a cleansing current.

down the presentation and try plastic baits again, fishing them in the dense cover.

As summer progresses into fall, the bass will be running bait, trying to fatten up for winter. Rat-L-Traps and spinnerbaits are effective then for the roaming schools of bass.

Winter bass are the most difficult to locate and catch on the river, according to Lazoen. With the waterway in the middle of continuing restoration, that shouldn't change. Fishing may be more difficult all year long as the waterway changes to a final state.

WHERE TO LOOK

Besides the obvious advantage of two to three times more fishable water with a restored river channel, the oxbows with current have greater depths. The current flow will keep the bottom clean, and that translates to more and better spawning areas. The diverse plant life now flourishes over a much wider area.

Slack water areas out of the main current are ideal for river largemouth. A bend in the river, or "oxbow" as it was destined to be known after channelization, may provide such quiet water. A stump or rooted system may also create a blockage and slack water behind it. The bass will get behind such structures and dart out into the current to feed. At rest, they can get out of the flow.

River fishing is primarily edge fishing. You are fishing the face of the cover along the bank. It may only be five feet deep and ten feet to hard ground. It is wise to search the river bends for masses of hydrocotyle, a vegetation that is rooted to the marshy bank and

61

forms floating canopies out over the surface of the water. Bass love to move in beneath the horizontal-growing vegetation, which offers plenty of shade and protection.

Hydrocotyle is prevalent on the river system, along with water hyacinths, water lettuce, hydrilla, bulrushes and cattails. Any time two plants are mixed, that's a good area to fish also. An area that has a mixture of hydrocotyle and pads is ideal.

Tapered points around the islands are often productive hot-weather bass haunts. Abrupt points and associated drops are usually good only if current flow exists. The shallow canals off the river are particularly good spots to fish in the spring. Those with sandy bottoms are magnets to spawning fish that want to move out of the currents. Topwater lures and jerk baits are most productive in such areas that may average only four feet deep.

Plentiful Largemouth

The summer months are most productive on the river. Lazoen has caught largemouth up to eight pounds then, and at other times has pulled in giants of 11 and 12 pounds. With the good depth and structure in the Kissimmee, along with excellent food, there is a good grade of bass living in those waters. Crayfish, shiners, chub minnows, crappie and bluegill keep trophy-size bass happy. In the river, the monsters are not common, though.

There are good numbers of bass in the river, and there will be days during the summer when an angler may catch 20 or 30 bass. When you find that type of fishing, however, the four and five pounders will be rare. The fish metabolism is higher in hot weather, and the smaller bass feed more often. Bass are frequently positioned on the straight edge walls provided by cattails and bulrushes. Those areas where hyacinths have blown in are then excellent fishing.

Lazoen is optimistic about the new fishing opportunities that will be provided by the entire restoration of the Kissimmee River.

"It'll get better," he points out. "Right now you have so many bass and when you double the amount of water, they can be in twice as many places. It is harder to catch them. Once they get established in the new waterway and have a few good spawns, the fishing will pick up dramatically in the river.

Bass angler Perry Lynn fished the river when he was just a kid before it was channeled, and he has noticed many changes over the years. It was much prettier in its original condition. There were

Fishing the varying terrain along the Kissimmee River as it runs beside the Avon Park Bombing Range can be interesting.

several swamp areas and backwaters then that filtered the flow from Lake Kissimmee to Okeechobee. The river was full of vegetation. That filtration is minimal now, and the old river just doesn't look natural any longer.

"I'm not sure they can fix it now," Lynn says. "How can they fix it when the DNR airboats go out each day and spray the old river channel's vegetation to kill it? To put it back the way it was, they need to leave the vegetation to help slow the river and to provide better filtration of pollutants."

RIVER AND RAMP DETAILS

One thing that may affect the Kissimmee River fisherman's peace and quiet along that stretch of the river is the neighbor. The three weirs lie at the eastern edge of the Avon Park Bombing Range. Sleek aircraft roar by overhead during many outings. The seemingly continuous supply of fighter jets pushing the speed of sound can make boat conversation difficult at times.

The wide C-38 canal is dredged so that a sheer dropoff exists on each side, away from the shoreline cover. The bottom along the canal varies from 8 to 30 feet, and often there is a double dropoff.

That can be determined with a depth finder or by noticing a change in plant growth.

In tight, you'll find hydrocotyle and other rooted plants that grow from the shore out. There could be joint grass or Kissimmee grass from the shore out, then there may be a drop, and you'll find lily pads or maybe, even bulrushes if the water has been clear. The next break or dropoff will be the final one to the maximum depth.

Loss of habitat and habitat diversity has caused large scale declines in fowl and game fish populations within the basin, according to Steven Miller, Game and Fresh Water Fish Commission biologist. The Project Leader of the Kissimmee River Restoration Evaluation Team has found restoration of flow in the three old river runs has already flushed out much of the siltation and created more favorable habitat for fish.

Miller points to a twofold increase in electrofishing catch rates of game species in Pool B last year as evidence that increased recruitment and production has resulted from the project. Other data from his evaluation of the test project suggests that water manipulation is vital to maintaining habitat quality in revitalized runs during the year. The esthetic values of the runs are greatly enhanced now, and Miller foresees additional fishery productivity for the oxbows.

There are seven launch ramps along the river between Lake Kissimmee and Lake Okeechobee. The South Florida Water Management District has a good map depicting the access points. Six locks and the three weirs can slow navigation along the 56 mile stretch. The weirs have navigation notches incorporated into each, and they will accommodate most large boats. Boaters should use extreme caution when traveling the waterway during dense fog or after dark. The massive steel weirs are well marked for normal vision situations, but caution should be used on the river. Signs are posted at approaches to each weir along with other safety aids.

Those wanting more information on the restoration can contact Miller at the Lake Okeechobee Fisheries Office, 3991 S.E. 27th Court, Okeechobee, FL 34974. Information on Lazoen's guide service can be obtained by writing him at 8 Prinville St., Port Charlotte, FL 33954 or call (813) 627-1704.

WINTER HAVEN CHAIN GANGS

OUR CASTS HIT adjacent pilings simultaneously. While I watched my line twitch once on the fall, my partner evidently also had a strike. Ray Rairigh and I set back on our rods at the same instant and the boat rocked slightly.

My bass headed for deep water while Ray's headed back under the dock. Our steady pressure on each fish resulted in quickly lipping that double. Both largemouth were chunky and easily exceeded two pounds. They were returned to the water to again take their position beneath the Lake Shipp dock.

The cypress trees, docks, cattails and vegetation variety in the Winter Haven Chain of Lakes are popular bass haunts in Polk County.

We continued to toss our plastic worms into the shade beneath the numerous piers and pile-supported docks on the relatively shallow waterway. Ray had another strike on his first cast to the adjacent dock and battled a much larger fish. He soon lifted a 4 1/2 pound largemouth from the water. That morning, like many late summer mornings, the bass were resting under the shady man-made wood structures.

On Lake Shipp, part of the South Winter Haven Chain of Lakes, the ramp isn't far from the hot-weather action under the wooden docks. While such structures are great fishing in hot weather, the nearby reed beds are difficult to top during the rest of the year.

Ray and I had a successful morning's fishing. Bass were evidently abundant, from our continuous action. In the first hour, we had a total of seven strikes and landed five. Over the following three hours, we each caught five more bass. We released all the fish.

The cattails and rushes in the Winter Haven Chain all yield largemouth during the spring and fall months.

Lake Shipp is, in fact, one of the chain's best bass waters, and the piers on its west shore have resulted in numerous successful trips for me. Hot weather moves bass into such structures, and the best bet for attraction is the plastic worm. Cast it several feet back under the docks for action. Allow the worms to flutter to the bottom in the four to six foot depths and then to sit motionless for up to a full minute. Generally, a largemouth will move over after 15 or 20 seconds and softly inhale the tasty-looking morsel.

Like Shipp, like the shorelines of most Winter Haven Chain lakes, is well-developed with housing and docks, yet restrictions on vegetation control prevents valuable habitat from being totally wiped out. The lack of profuse aquatic plant communities, however, has forced the Game and Fresh Water Fish Commission to place five fish attractors in the two chains. The attractors cover an area of approximately 100 feet by 100 feet and are marked by floating buoys. Lakes Eloise, Hartridge and Summit in the South Chain each have one and Lake Rochelle in the North Chain has two.

The Commission also completed a study of bass populations on the Winter Haven Chain which had promising results. The study revealed that Lakes Winterset, Shipp, Howard, Cannon and Lulu had excellent numbers of bass. Lakes Winterset and Eloise had the largest average size of largemouth, while Hartridge had more small bass.

Any way to maintain or improve the fishery on this "active" chain is surely appreciated by anglers. There are numerous water activities on the South Chain, some of which are not conducive to

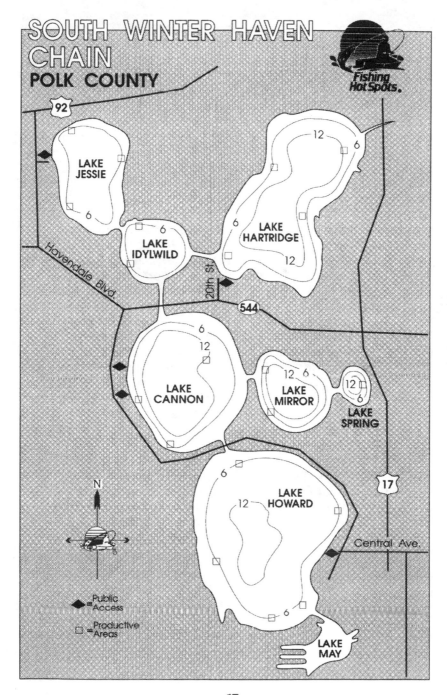

SOUTH WINTER HAVEN
CHAIN
POLK COUNTY

Fishing Hot Spots.

92

LAKE JESSIE

6

12 6

LAKE HARTRIDGE

6

12

Havendale Blvd

6

LAKE IDYLWILD

20th St

544

6

12

LAKE CANNON

12 6

LAKE MIRROR

12

LAKE SPRING

6

LAKE HOWARD

12

17

Central Ave.

N

◆ = Public Access

□ = Productive Areas

6

LAKE MAY

67

angling success. Skiers often scoot around the lakes and even fly overhead on their kites. Water skiing is popular on several of the lakes and is allowed on all lakes, but some restrictions on parasailing exist on lakes near airports.

The home of the famous tourist attraction, Cypress Gardens, is on the shores of Lake Eloise. The Cypress Gardens water ski show takes place there, and a small portion of the lake in front of the attraction's grand stand is off-limits to the public. Marker buoys define that area. Boaters are allowed to watch the shows from the water as long as they remain outside those markers. Its "Island In The Sky" overlooks the lake and helps make these pretty waters one of the most photographed in the country. Fortunately for those interested in the esthetic value of a fishing trip, there is still plenty of wildlife around these waters and others in the chain.

Access between lakes is by interconnecting canals, although a drought can make navigation difficult for larger boats. With summer thunderstorms common, that's not usually a problem then. Most of the lakes have launch ramps and other facilities. Gas is available only on the larger waters, and food may be a short drive away from most lakes. On Lake Shipp, one of my favorite restaurants is Harborside, which is right on the water.

The lakes were connected into a chain in 1915 by a group of Winter Haven boaters who called themselves the "20 Lake Boat Club." But a lack of finances prevented the club from being able to keep the canals in good shape, so the chain went public in 1919. Winter Haven residents pay taxes to the Region Boat Course District to maintain the waterways today, and they seldom complain about these taxes.

Without the canals, the lakes would be just isolated bodies of water, just like about 80 other lakes within a 10-mile radius of the city. With canals, the lakes take on a different meaning. Each lake in the chain has its own personality and bass fishing activities.

TACTICS, LURES & BAIT

Worming the cattails and docks on the chains can be very effective during hot weather. Productive anglers will toss scented plastic worms when the sun is overhead. The bright, hot weather moves bass into the shady structures.

Docks on the two chains come in all shapes, sizes, lengths and conditions. Some have small cabins or boat houses on the end of the pier, and others are partially dilapidated. Most are wooden,

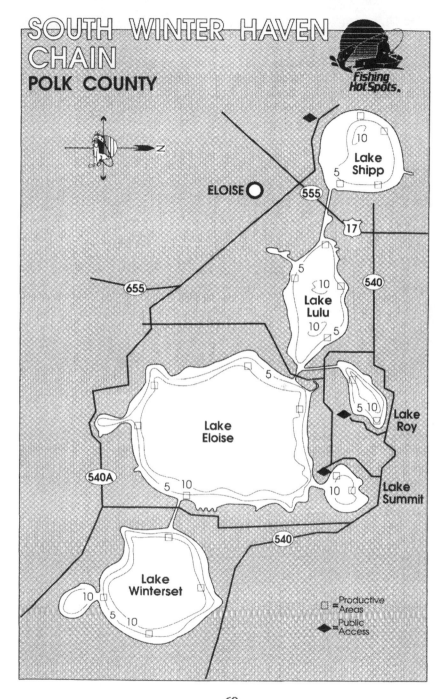

SOUTH WINTER HAVEN CHAIN
POLK COUNTY

Fishing Hot Spots,

ELOISE ○

555

17

Lake Shipp

10
5

655

540

5
10
Lake Lulu
10
5

540A

5
Lake Eloise

5 10
Lake Roy

5 10

10
Lake Summit

540

10
5 10
Lake Winterset

□ = Productive Areas

◆ = Public Access

but a few metal piers and posts can occasionally be found. The best pier to locate bass under will depend on several things, but the most important characteristic is how close it is to deep water. The piers on which small houses are built provide excellent bass fishing. The wider piers which cast a wider shadow are prime territories.

Another consideration in selecting the dock to fish is the density and size of the support posts. The more dense (number of posts, cross-members near the water, etc.) the more productive a pier can be. The larger in diameter that these posts are, the better they usually prove to be also.

Most lakes in the two chains are lined with cattails or bulrushes. Such vegetation is a prime area for giant largemouth and the flippin' technique is often successful on these waters. A plastic worm with 3/8 ounce bullet weight, or a jig and plastic trailer, is gently flipped under a low-slung dock or into a hole of heavy cover adjacent to the man-made structure in hopes of pulling out a trophy bass.

Casting the submergent vegetation in deeper water is also productive, and deep-diving crankbaits and vibrating plugs are the ticket. Fish them around the bass habitat and near the bottom during the cooler times. While some bass move from deep water in the summer and winter to the shoreline, others remain in open water around submerged vegetation. Use vibrating plugs, like the Rat-L-Trap, on the outer edges of the cover, in boat lanes and over the submergent vegetation.

When the waters cool, bass will be in deeper waters adjacent to good sandy spawning areas. Toss a deep-running crankbait and work it slowly along the bottom, near structure. Slow-rolling spinnerbaits along the deeper edges of vegetation can be effective also. For trophy bass on the two Winter Haven Chains, fish during the winter months. Try slow, big baits or live shiners.

Where To Look - South

On Lake Shipp, the cattails in three to six feet of water are home to largemouth in the spring and early summer. Docks, wooden piers and boat houses on the lake hold bass in high sun times, and open water bass can be taken in the summer around Lake Shipp's 12 foot breakline. To the south, the pilings supporting the Highway 17 overpass and nearby railroad bridge can hold bass when boat traffic is minimal.

On Lake Lulu, further south in the chain, hot-weather fishing on the 8 and 10 foot breaklines, particularly those with mussel bars

The cypress knees in Lake Eloise can be the home of many bass during cooler weather.

on them, and around the boat docks in six feet of water can be productive. Fishing the docks with profuse reed growth adjacent on the east shoreline of the lake is best. Bass inhabit the man-made structures on the firm sand bottom.

Lake Eloise bass sometimes hang out in the deep holes offshore during the summer. Fish the cypress trees in shallow water, and then try the lake's deep holes for trophy largemouth. Check out the eel grass beds and reed patches in 3 to 5 feet of water in the spring and fall. Brush sunk around many docks in Eloise often goes virtually unnoticed.

Lake Winterset is a deep lake, and its breaklines at 10 and 20 feet are productive in the summer and winter months. One hole that yields summer bass is 25 feet deep. Little Lake Winterset is a tiny, deep lake off Lake Winterset. It has several good dropoffs, particularly along the eastern shoreline.

Two other small lakes on the southern end of the chain are Lakes Roy and Summit. A 25 foot hole in Roy attracts summer largemouth, and the dense cattails and grass are good spring and fall spots. In Lake Summit, the remains of an old fish attractor in 15 feet of water often produce bass. Several submerged trees still litter the bottom in this area. The cattails along the eastern shoreline attract bass in the spring and early summer.

On the north end of the chain lies Lake Hartridge and some excellent eel grass and hydrilla breaklines in 10 feet of water. This

71

area is an excellent schooling largemouth and sunshine bass spot in the fall months. Also cast to the sparse hydrilla and eel grass cover around the lake's fish attractor. Little Lake Idylwild, just west of Hartridge, has some deep structure and eel grass to fish, in addition to cattails and scattered pads and peppergrass.

Nearby Lake Jessie's summer largemouth are often taken from drops in 10 feet of water or from the numerous boat docks and adjacent dense grass in five feet of water. Lake Jessie's boat houses on the northeast side overlooking the airport are especially productive. Lake Cannon offers some open-water mussel bar fishing along 12 to 14 foot drops, if you can find the mussel bar. An old dock area off the southeast shoreline of Cannon between Lake Mirror and Lake Howard canals can be very productive. A canal on the east side leads to Lake Mirror and a productive deep hole.

Lake Howard offers good fishing around the boat docks and eel grass patches in the summer months. Fish the dense cattails and sparse grass in 3 to 6 feet of water from the fall through the early summer. In the middle of the lake, summertime bass can often be caught from the drops. Just south, tiny Lake May has some productive canals, a good breakline in 6 to 10 feet of water and some shallow cattails to try in the fall and spring.

Where To Look - North

The North Winter Haven Chain often has low water, and getting a bass boat through the interconnecting canals can be difficult. As a result, this chain has less fishing pressure on it and several overlooked, yet productive areas where largemouth may be abundant. On Lake Rochelle, for example, a couple of fish attractors, one old and one relatively new, often yield bass. The submerged cover on the west and east end of the lake can be especially productive during the hotter months. The same holds true for the 10-foot breakline on the southern side then and for the cattails in shallow water in the spring.

Big Lake Haines produces bass from its stretches of grass and scattered cattails on the west and south shores and along the breakline in eight to 10 feet of water on the east side.

The twin "water-bubbles" of Conine and Smart also have good bassin' areas. In fact, the largest bass from the North Winter Haven Chain are often taken out of Lake Conine. With its cattail border in two to four feet of water, Conine is usually considered the best flippin' territory in this chain. The sharp 20 foot drop-off

72

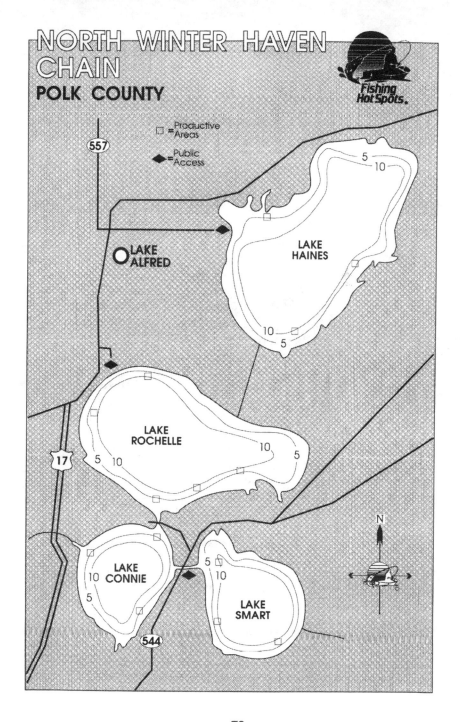

NORTH WINTER HAVEN CHAIN
POLK COUNTY

☐ = Productive Areas

◆ = Public Access

557

LAKE ALFRED

LAKE HAINES

5
10

10
5

LAKE ROCHELLE

17

5
10

10
5

LAKE CONNIE

10

5

LAKE SMART

5
10

N

544

Fish the docks on this chain for bass action in the summer months.

near its south shore should be checked out. On Smart, wise bassers will try the cattails in three feet of water on the west shoreline, any mussel bars in 10 foot depths off the southern end of the lake, and the 10 foot breakline off the eastern bank.

CHAIN DETAILS

The South Winter Haven Chain consists of 14 beautiful, interconnected lakes of about 4,400 acres. The North Winter Haven Chain is small in comparison, consisting of 4 interconnected lakes encompassing some 1,825 acres. The South Chain is developed with residential communities on most of the shorelines. The North Chain, located on the north side of the city, has less development and more wetland shoreline on its lakes.

Winter Haven is a city of canals and lakes, including this popular chain. The canals between the lakes on the two chains are no-wake zones, and they are strictly enforced. While the lakes are natural, several holes have been dredged in most of them. These small and isolated holes, dug to get at fill dirt for adjacent residential development, are the deepest waters in each lake.

A canal which used to connect the North and South Chain is blocked. Inflow to all of the connected waters in the two chains is primarily from watershed runoff. Lake Spring and a few others have minimal spring influence. The water color varies some from one lake to another. Tannic-stained waters exist in most lakes on both chains. Lake Hartridge, which is very clear with visibility of six to seven feet, and Lakes Spring and Idylwild, which also have good clarity, are the exceptions.

Most of the lakes in the both chains have minimal offshore vegetation. Lakes Hartridge, Cannon, Howard, Shipp, Roy, Eloise and Idylwild have some eel grass. Hydrilla is most abundant in

74

South Winter Haven Chain			
Lake	Acreage	Max. Depth	Avg. Depth
Hartridge	434	25	15
Idylwild	102	15	10
Jessie	190	15	10
Mirror	123	16	13
Cannon	336	18	14
Spring	25	25	20
Howard	628	20	12
May	44	10	7
Shipp	283	15	10
Lulu	301	10	8
Roy	78	25	15
Summit	68	20	15
Eloise	1,160	25	18
Winterset	548	30	22
Little Winterset	*	30	22
* acreage included in Lake Winterset			

North Winter Haven Chain			
Lake	Acreage	Max. Depth	Avg. Depth
Haines	716	18	14
Rochelle	578	18	14
Conine	236	30	12
Smart	275	15	12

Lakes Hartridge and Roy. Some maidencane can be found in Lakes Shipp and Winterset and elsewhere in the South Chain.

Moderately abundant along the shorelines of almost all lakes are bulrushes, reeds and cattails. They are emergent-type vegetation which can attain heights up to seven feet. Dense stands of cattails tight to the shore in extremely shallow waters provide some benefit to the chain's fishery, since the vegetation helps remove excess nutrients flowing into the lakes. Lake Eloise has numerous cypress trees which also provide cover.

RAMP AND GUIDE DETAILS

There are seven public ramps on the South Winter Haven Chain. On the west side of Lake Jessie off Idylwild Drive NW and Biltmore Drive West is the Lake Jessie ramp. On the southwest side of Lake Hartridge off Highway 544 (Havendale Boulevard) and 20th Street is the Lake Hartridge ramp. On the west side of Lake Cannon off 24th St. NW and Lake Cannon Drive are two public ramps.

Lake Howard's public ramp is located on the east side at the Lake Howard City Pier and Winter Haven City Park. You can access it off Highway 17 and Central Ave. On the south side of Lake Shipp off Highway 655 (Recker Highway) is the chain's most popular facility. On the south side of Lake Roy off Highway 540 (Cypress Gardens Boulevard) and Lake Roy Drive is the Lake Roy ramp. Another Polk County park with ramp is located on the west side of Lake Summit off Highway 540 and West Lake Summit Dr.

There are three public ramps on the North Winter Haven Chain. One is on the east side of Lake Conine off Highway 544; a second one lies on the northwest side of Lake Rochelle off Highway 17/92, and the third is on the west side of Lake Haines on Haines Boulevard.

For more information on the chain, contact the Winter Haven Chamber of Commerce. For information on the area waters, contact the Polk Country Tourist Development Council. Guide service on the chain is available from Professional Bass Guide Service, Dave Hoy, P.O. Box 91663, Lakeland, FL 33804-1663, phone (813) 533-3865; and from Carroll Hagood at phone (813) 967-8097.

8

POLK COUNTY'S CATTAIL BASS

MY GUIDE FRIEND let out a yelp as he set the hook into a two-pound bass. The fish flew out of the water beside the cattails and was grabbed by Dave Hoy in mid-air. Blackie Lightfoot and I watched from nearby.

"Flip your worms into the weeds," Dave reiterated. "Just work the pockets and holes."

Flippin' is a deadly method on Lakeland's Lake Parker and Dave is one of the top guides in South Central Florida, but the boat operator and his partner must be in sync when using the short-line method. Blackie's heart was not in flippin' worms that morning. His interest was in twitching a Bomber "Long A" around the masses of vegetation that covered most every foot of Lake Parker's perimeter.

Some of the least-known lakes in Florida's largest county are the most productive.

We worked a Texas-rigged worm into and out of several holes in the dense stands of cattails, per Dave's instruction, but it was to no avail. I continued flipping the emergent cover but Blackie's boat was moving away from the structure. It was a long reach for me, even with 7 foot rod and well-practiced swing cast. I looked up to see that Blackie was working his minnow plug through the shallow waters ahead.

A largemouth jumped on his plug after the second twitch, and Blackie's lightweight rod bent almost double with the weight of a fat 2 1/2 pound fish. A second fish on his next cast further commanded my attention, and after another two swirls which missed, I decided to join in on the fun.

"Want one of these Long A's?," Blackie queried.

Not being overly in love with one particular lure type, I accepted his generosity and tied on an identical plug. Blackie's third bass was taken 50 yards down the shoreline between an offshore weed mass and those along the lake's perimeter. I made about a dozen casts before noticing a cut in the cattail bed on the deep water side.

I tossed the Long A to the mouth of the cut, twitched it three times and started a steady retrieve back to the boat. The lure didn't get far. The heavyweight bass simply stopped the lure's forward momentum. Feeling the resistance, I set the hook and, immediately, a huge bass took to the air. Three jumps later, she neared boatside. Carefully, I pulled her within Blackie's reach.

"Ten pounds," he said hauling the fat female aboard. "Beautiful fish! I told you that lure would get us a big one."

Dave had watched the tussle from his nearby boat and came over to inspect the fish. The 25 inch long fish was appreciated by all. It was photographed and released. While Dave continued flipping worms into his favorite spots on Parker, we stuck with our jerk baits. All of us caught another four or five bass by our departure time at high noon.

Lake Parker is often kind to expert fishermen like guide Dave Hoy. Sometimes, though, fishing can run hot one day and cold the next. The lake, located between Highway 92 and Interstate 4, has two power plants on its bank and fishing around them can be especially productive in cold weather. Lake level fluctuations are held to a minimum to accommodate the power plant water needs.

Parker covers 2,272 acres and is connected to a few old phosphate pits. Fishing in them can be exciting at times. One of them, Lake Crago, lies just off S.R. 33 and is almost 60 acres. It receives plenty of pressure, but the old pit does produce good bass fishing. Boaters can launch from a small dirt ramp or motor over from Lake Parker. For maximum action, fish the submerged bars in open water, anchor over a drop and fish a plastic worm slowly, or employ a deep-running crankbait during the summer months.

A lot of big bass swim in the excellent aquatic habitat in Lake Parker and its adjacent phosphate pits. Casting the rushes and cattails early, then moving against them to 'flip' plastic worms is often most productive for big largemouth. Moving further inside the cattails and 'flippin' the really dense stuff is often necessary in the heat of summer. Black with chartreuse tail, pumpkinseed, moccasin and red shad are prime color combos for the flippin' worm fare on Parker.

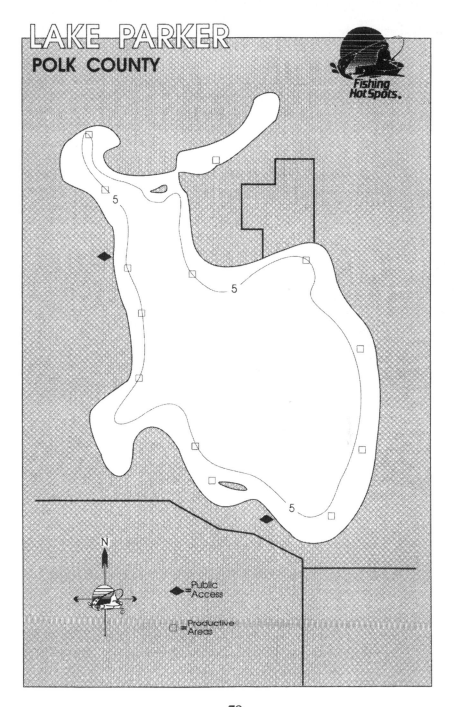

LAKE PARKER

POLK COUNTY

Fishing
Hot Spots.

N

◆ = Public
Access

□ = Productive
Areas

A couple of miles away lies Lake Hunter, the Lakeland city waterhole that was restored in 1984. It has quickly developed into a flourishing fishery. The lake, located west of Highway 37, was drawn down for a biological cleanup and refilled. Results of the restoration project have been encouraging. The size of bass found in Game & Fresh Water Fish Commission samplings is significant.

Not all of Hunter's thriving population was a result of stocking after the lake was refilled. Apparently, there were a few left in the tiny puddle of water remaining after drawdown. The largemouth bass have a blossoming fishery in a lake no longer polluted. Lake Hunter is a healthy body that should remain so for many years now. Access is limited to shore fishing and small cartoppers, but no parking is allowed on the grass.

Lake Hollingsworth, located just south of downtown Lakeland near the Florida Southern College campus, is a good bass water that is often overlooked by area anglers. The college, designed by Frank Lloyd Wright, is on the northern side and that area just off the steep bank is one of the lake's best. Bass move into the pads there from nearby deep water.

The only public ramp lies in the city park on Hollingsworth's southern shoreline adjacent to the Lakeland Yacht Club. The lake is a little less than three miles in circumference, and bicyclers, joggers, strollers and automobile cruisers have taken more than a passing interest in the scenic waters. Water skiers frequent the lake in warm weather months, but, somewhat surprisingly, even they are not over abundant.

Restoration of beneficial aquatic plants occurred a few years ago after most perimeter cattails and lily pads, out of control at the time, had been "eaten" by a couple of mechanical harvesters. Today, the lake has pencil rushes and other vegetation that lends itself to productive flippin'. While flippin' is very effective on Hollingsworth, so is swimming plastic worms and spoons through the pads in three feet of water.

Texas-rigged worms with "pegged" slip sinker are normally most effective early and late in the day. Insert a toothpick point into the weight hole beside the line and break it off to wedge the sinker to the line and prevent it from sliding up and down. That translates to better control of the rig as it is being placed in a pothole beside the rush stalks, jigged up and down, and then moved to another opening nearby.

Many giant bass are taken from Polk County lakes in the spring and summer months.

DRIFTING FOR BASS

The clear, tea-colored water of Lake Mattie engulfs cattails, cypress trees, and other aquatic vegetation. The natural lake with an implant of state fish attractors is just two miles around and lies just south of Polk City and I-4, about eight miles northeast of Lakeland. There are no ramps on the lake, but access is available through a canal on the east side of Lake Juliana, near Auburndale.

Drifting dark plastic worms, with curl tails, in open water can be very productive here. Red, chartreuse, and pink on a smoke or glitter worm in a 7-inch length can be deadly. Let the wind push the boat through the open area and use 12 pound test line with a 1/4 ounce bullet weight to keep the drifting worm in contact with the bottom. During high winds, use a sea anchor to slow the boat and trailing bait.

The same "drifting open water" technique is effective on nearby Lake Juliana. The lake offers clear water with cattails, sawgrass, and patches of hydrilla. It gives up quite a number of smaller bass. Fish attractors on Juliana congregate some bass for those not wishing to search open water for them. There are no public ramps on the lake, but there are two private fish camps with launch fees.

Another productive technique is "yo-yoing" Rat-L-Traps over the highly vegetated lake bottom. Such tactics work on schools of bass located in the depths. The bass in Juliana, Lake Mattie and nearby Lake Ariana, tend to relate to depth in the clear waters, and that's why they are often found offshore. Any "roughage" along the lake bottom, such as rock or hydrilla, will concentrate the fish.

81

Ariana, where periodically "hot" fishing exists, is a 1,000 acre lake with access through a City of Auburndale ramp. It is located adjacent to the city beach on the southwest shore. The lake offers particularly good bass action in the summer and fall months.

Nearby, Lake Arietta can yield bass to 13 pounds. Also known as "Lake Lighterlog," this clear water with cattails, sawgrass, and patches of hydrilla gives up quite a number of smaller bass. No public access is currently available to the round-shaped water.

Carroll Hagood of Auburndale is a professional fisherman and guide on Juliana, Ariana and other area lakes. He does a great job of putting anglers on big bass. I fished with him on a warm May day for about three hours and caught three healthy bass, including one almost 10 pounds. We fished the plastic tube-type baits in hydrilla-infested waters about seven to nine feet deep.

AREA TOPOGRAPHY AND GIANTS

Most of the area's natural lakes average 10 to 12 feet in depth and are lined with cattails and grass beds. They range in size from a few acres to several hundred. Many are surrounded by residential areas or office parks in a few cases, but most have some natural topography present along some of the shorelines. A few on the edges of town are adjoining citrus groves. When the orange blossoms burst forth in the late spring, those are the most "perfumed" waters around.

Some Polk County waters have stands of cypress that have clung to their natural foothold, despite the encroachment of civilization. Many of the lakes have paved roads to their shores, while some may offer access to those with a small cartopper boat transported down a sandy back road. Ramps, dirt in some cases and concrete in others, vary widely in state and condition.

A truck or 4-wheel drive vehicle occasionally may be required for the remote spots. Gas is available only on the larger waters and food may be a short drive away from most lakes. You won't use too many gallons of fuel either.

Lake records on most Polk County waters are in the mid to upper teens. Some records are new, while many have stood for several years. For example, I've seen ancient pictures of two men holding 15 bass caught from Lakeland's Lake Parker. All the fish appeared to be over 12 pounds! Regardless of when lake largemouth records were set or huge stringers were landed and photographed, many of the Polk County lakes currently produce nice stringers of bass with an occasional specimen over the 10-pound mark.

Shorelines of small and mid-size lakes in the county offer some development as well as natural terrain.

BOULEVARD ACTION

Fishing beside a busy highway can have surprising results, as I found out on my first trip to Lake Parker eight years ago. I had just launched by boat at the public ramp on the southern shore off State Road 92 (Memorial Boulevard). Flippin' as a method of dropping worms into vegetation beside the boat had just started to gain recognition as being highly successful in South Florida waters. A huge stand of cattails were growing beside the ramp, so I thought I'd try to flip the dense cover.

I dropped the trolling motor and moved the boat closer to the stalks that towered above me. Cars roared by on the busy highway. My bulky worm had checked out three holes in the vegetation before finding a bass at home. It grabbed the bait on the fall and shouldered its way through the emergent stalks into cover even more dense. Steady pressure resulted in a giant-size boil in the weed mass and a "crack" as my line parted.

Laying down the casting outfit with 17 pound test, I picked up one with 20. Soon, it was rigged with the right bait and employed. I hadn't moved over 50 feet before another weed-bound Parker bass tried to make off with the worm. I set the hook and horsed out a two pounder. It bounced off my chest and fell into the boat without the now dangling hook and worm rig. The fish was startled, probably, but my hook sets had been accompanied by bass flying into and over the boat before. In fact, I have lost several that I moved from one side of the boat to the other, the hook becoming free in mid-air.

I quickly grabbed that largemouth and moved her about in the water to wash off any boat "dust" her ride might have gathered. She swam away none the worse for wear. The new worm was placed not two feet away, on the other side of that cattail clump. As I lifted it up from the bottom, something felt peculiar. I let the bait fall, but it didn't.

Immediately, I swung the rod upward expecting another bass to come flinging out of the jungle habitat. This fish wouldn't have that, and started to move back into the vegetation. I snubbed her and forced her back toward the boat where she rammed the side. The eight pounder tore up some weed bed just off the gunwale, but I finally stuck my thumb into her mouth.

My partner took a few pictures of the beauty, taking great care to crop out the traffic on the nearby highway in the camera's viewfinder, and I released her. Within another hundred yards along the cattails adjacent to Highway 92, we each had another heavyweight bass. Mine weighed just over six pounds on a small spring scale and the other was slightly smaller. Three largemouth and another six missed strikes later, we loaded the boat and headed home. I gained a lot of respect for Lake Parker that day and even forgot about the roadside noise while fishing the great cover there.

SMALL HONEY HOLES

While Polk County's behemoths Lake Kissimmee and Lake Hatchineha, and its famous phosphate pits, grab most of the attention in this part of the bass world, many excellent small waters exist. They are every bit as good as the "big boys." The great bass fishing in the small natural lakes of Polk County goes virtually unnoticed, until local anglers "discover" it.

Lake Gibson on the north side of Lakeland not far from Interstate 4 has its share of residences and boat traffic from skiers, sail boaters and fishermen. It also has plenty of bass, including some whoppers. An abundance of grass around the shore is good bass habitat, where anglers often flip worms. Use a slightly lighter weight on Gibson for best results along the grass edges. Some deep water structure exists on the lake, and anglers will find it with their depth finders. Access is provided by a ramp in Lake Gibson Park off North Socrum Loop Road near the interstate.

Saddle Creek Park, located on the east side of the city on Highway 92, can offer fair to good bass fishing. The 740-acre park has numerous man-dug lakes that total over 500 acres. The areas

Lake Parker yields lots of heavyweight bass to a variety of lures and techniques.

A more significant catch occurred years later. Rhoden was on his way home from work when he decided to fish Buffum despite a 30 mph northeast wind. A hurricane was off the Daytona coast some 70 miles away as the younger Rhoden tossed plastic worms that evening, just before sundown. He had waded out into Buffum's shallows and within 15 minutes caught two giant bass. The smallest weighed 11-pounds, 10-ounces and the real whopper pulled the scales down to 15-pounds, 7-ounces. The biggest (landed) measured 30 inches and although caught in the fall, appeared to have recently dropped its eggs. He stated that an even larger one got away!

Buffum is not normally a productive lake for numbers of bass, according to Rhoden. It is, as many small waters are, hit or miss. Shortly after the two big fish were taken from those waters, several local bass club tournaments were held there. With success on tournament-size fish minimal, that fishing pressure quickly diminished. Buffum has a fish attractor which can yield an occasional trophy bass. Other tiny lakes in the vicinity also have some monsters in them.

NAMELESS WATERS

A monster largemouth bass weighing almost 18 pounds was taken from a small, natural lake in Polk County at a time when females of significant size are seldom caught. Bill Oberry, a 20-year resident of Seffner, wrestled the trophy to the boat during the July heat a few years ago.

The giant bass, measuring 30 inches in length and 22 1/2 inches in girth, hit a yellow/green skirted spinnerbait falling from a clump of maidencane into eight feet of water. The fish immediately swam away from the grass shoreline toward Oberry's aluminum boat. It never jumped but frequently spun the boat during the battle.

The 14-pound mono held and his wife netted the fish. It was weighed some five hours later at a tackle shop, but certified two days later after it had been frozen. The "official" weight,17-pounds, four ounces, was still good enough to become a new "certified" state record bass (the "non-certified" record stands at 20-pounds, two ounces). The lake that Oberry is reluctant to name has several deep holes, which is unusual for waters in the state.

Most of the county area north of I-4 is called the Green Swamp and is void of public named lakes, but go south and Polk County is extremely hard to beat for top bass action. Weekends are often busy for area lakes, but while water skiers may be numerous, anglers can always find a worming spot along a weeded shoreline.

The proximity of one Polk County lake to another is important and if the fish aren't 'biting' on one, it is generally a few miles travel down the road or down a canal to another lake that might be turned-on. Small waters are numerous and an afternoon trip before the sun goes down is often possible for the nearby locals.

Lake and Guide Details

For details on Saddle Creek Park, the best source is Phillips Bait and Tackle on Highway 92 adjacent the park. For more information on the lakes of Polk County, contact guides Dave Hoy at (813)533-3865; or Carroll Hagood at (813)967-8097. For information on Lakes Pierce and others in the southeastern part of the county, contact the Lake Wales Area Chamber of Commerce.

For further information on area waters, contact the Game & Fresh Water Fish Commission South Region. A free brochure listing county-maintained boat ramps and lakeside parks is available from the Polk County Parks & Recreation at (813)534-6000.

9

PHOSPHATE PIT BONANZAS

"THIS POINT HAS a bar coming off it, and it drops off from 12 feet down to about 20 on each side," Jim Porter explained, as he positioned the boat and readied his crankbait for a cast. "A crank plug is usually the key to taking fish off this submerged structure. Throw your bait..."

He never finished his statement. The avid angler set back on his rod and we both watched the angle of the taut line increase, as the fish headed to the surface. Porter kept pressure on the bass as it leaped through the surface with crankbait firmly attached.

Largemouth action in the pits of Tenoroc and other man-dug waters can be exciting!

"Small one," he mumbled, as he led the largemouth to the gunwale. "There should be bigger fish here on this drop."

The 2 1/2 pound Tenoroc bass was relieved of its lip "jewelry" and allowed to swim away. The bass put up a respectable fight and I was impressed with Porter's correct call about there being bass on the bar ready to hit a crankbait. An even smaller bass was the only other interested predator on that piece of bottom, so we were soon boating on to additional structures.

"In order to catch big bass or lots of bass on these pits, you have to fish deep," says Porter. "The average fisherman will come to the Reserve and cast the shorelines. They'll catch a few fish, but most of the big ones are deep. That's where the concentration of largemouth can be found."

The Palm Bay resident has trailed his boat to the pits at the Tenoroc State Reserve Fish Management Area, near Lakeland, numerous times over the past four years. He is familiar with the bottom structure in many of the Reserve's nine pits and has caught thousands of bass from them. A depth finder aids in locating the abundant deep humps and dropoffs that exist in most of the man-dug waters of Tenoroc.

My experience on those waters and numerous other phosphate pits has been similar. Most of my bass catches have come from deep structures, bottom elevation changes, rocks, dropoffs, etc. In fact, that may be the only way to find concentrations of bass in those waters, which range in size from 20 to over 250 acres. While most have irregular shorelines with some emergent vegetation to toss a lure at, I prefer fishing the more productive depths.

Tenoroc's Lake B, one of the initial pits opened in 1983 on a permit basis to all anglers, has little in the way of extensive shoreline habitat. Cattails, parrot's feather, and grasses were scattered along the shoreline. Some patches of hydrilla existed, but for the most part, they have been chemically-treated, or "sprayed clean," as some anglers grudgingly say. With very little dense vegetation in the Reserve's lakes and many other pits, anglers must utilize structure fishing techniques to capitalize on the deep water bass concentrations.

TENOROC OPPORTUNITIES

For those willing to spend time searching the depths for bottom changes, Tenoroc offers some of the best phosphate pit fishing available. Strict fishing regulations on the nine lakes currently open have maintained a quality bass fishery. Regulations do change occasionally, so check with the Reserve office for the latest. Catch and release restrictions now exist on three lakes, while slot limits and minimum length limits are in force on others.

Families can fish any of the waters, and Lake 2 has been set aside specifically for children and parents fishing from boats. To fish this lake, an adult must be accompanied by at least one person 15 years of age or younger. Anglers of all skill levels have enjoyed the quality fisheries. Current regulations on all lakes limit the number of boats and bank fishermen, as well as the fishing hours to daylight Thursday through Sunday by permit.

While many of the area's phosphate pits are private and off-limits to the public, Tenoroc offers everyone an opportunity to sample pit fishing. The popularity of old phosphate mines and the location's proximity to Lakeland ensures plenty of pressure, but angler quotas are seldom reached on all waters. The two most popular lakes are Lake B and Lake 5, and advance reservations are generally needed to access them early in the day. Hydrilla Lake is

This 16-pound Tenoroc bass was shocked up by Game and Fresh Water Fish Commission biologists and quickly released.

set aside for fly rod fishermen using artificials only. Seldom, if ever, has it filled the ten boat quota.

TACTICS, LURES & BAIT

I tossed both crankbaits and Texas-rigged plastic fare while Porter alternated between his two favorites, a small crankbait and a Carolina-rigged, 4-inch worm. For those not familiar with the latter, the rig consists of a 1/2 ounce egg sinker above a ball bearing swivel. Attached at the terminal end is an 18 inch long leader and a thin double-hook, straight-tail worm. Sliders, do-nothin's and limit-finders are some of the names that manufacturers tag on them. The bait tends to float up above the sinker that may be digging a trench across a soft, mucky bottom.

Lake 5 is fairly productive using Texas-rigged worms. There, I'll fish the extensions of points and under the overhanging trees. The few areas with rushes can be particularly productive for the worm tosser. Vibrating plugs, like the Rat-L-Trap, can be effective when tossed along the irregular shoreline. Hangups are not uncommon when you are fishing where the bass are.

Crankbaits were my tools on that lake a few years ago when the Florida Outdoor Writers Association had a tournament. Some 60 members were scattered throughout five of the Tenoroc pits. My five bass caught on Norman's Big N's weighed around 14 pounds and placed me third.

A worm assortment ideal for most pits would include pumpkinseed, brown, black, red shad, blue with silver glitter, moccasin and grape with blue glitter. The shad kill on pit waters is minimal during most winters, so a silver or bone-finish crankbait will catch plenty of bass if fished in the right place.

WHERE TO LOOK

Lake 5 and the others at Tenoroc vary considerably in topography, but are fairly typical of most phosphate pits. Some are pastureland type waters with very little shoreline cover, while others are completely unreclaimed and provide craggy outcroppings, heavy brush and trees along the shoreline and rocks jutting above the surface.

Most Reserve pits have an irregular shoreline and offer steep banks to cast toward. Very few shallow areas are found in the pits, and that is one reason why aquatic vegetation may be minimal. Waters in most of the lakes on the reserve are of medium clarity, but occasionally one may be found with fairly clear water. Many have rocks, sand and gravel outcropping along their bottom.

The bottom structures are places that Florida bass become adapted to quickly. Brush structure is abundant along the lake bottom in some of the pits. Overgrown islands exist, and "cuts" in the islands are excellent spots to fish, since the largemouth generally lay off such areas looking for a school of bait fish to swim over from the other side.

TROPHY CHANCES

Tenoroc, Florida's first experimental fish management area, has lots of lunker opportunities. A couple of years ago, Game and Fresh Water Commission personnel electro-shocked a 16-pound largemouth bass from the reserve's Lake B. The prespawn female was one of the two largest bass ever shocked by fisheries biologists.

While most really big largemouth are in deep waters which are difficult to effectively electro-shock, this fish was "sun bathing" over one of the four fish attractors installed in the pit. The monster was evidently above the 7-foot high pile of dead citrus trees in 10 feet of water. That precarious location made her vulnerable to the fisheries' generator equipment.

Lake B is the noted big bass water on the refuge. Over a one-year period, it yielded 29 bass over 22 inches in length to lucky anglers, according to project biologist, Phil Chapman. Several huge bass have been taken from the pit, and others have been caught and released back into those waters. One man has personally caught over 30 bass larger than 10 pounds from two of the lakes on the Reserve. He kept only three for a wall mount.

The biggest bass caught and released, though, was one that weighed over 15 pounds. It was caught on a worm fished along one of the humps. Such a fish would be hard for many anglers to

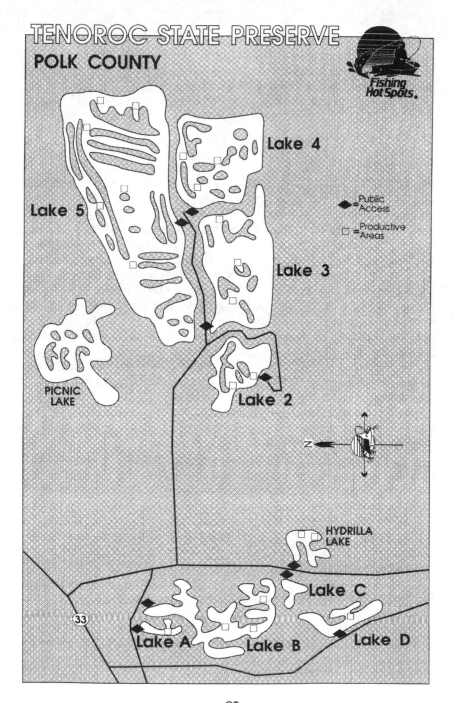

TENOROC STATE PRESERVE

POLK COUNTY

Lake 4

Lake 5

◆ = Public Access

□ = Productive Areas

Lake 3

PICNIC LAKE

Lake 2

N

HYDRILLA LAKE

Lake C

33

Lake A

Lake B

Lake D

release, but the man, whose largest prior to that was 7 1/2 pounds, watched the healthy fish swim off after several photos.

Big bass on other Tenoroc lakes do exist, and many 10-pound plus fish have been reported. Many pits have produced bass over 13 pounds, but seldom does the word get out in which pit the lunker is caught. The lucky anglers are usually pretty tight lipped.

RESERVE MANAGEMENT

The Tenoroc Fish Management Area is proof of the value of strict fishing regulations. Quality bass angling has been maintained since the beginning of the joint Game and Fresh Water Fish Commission and Department of Natural Resources project. One of the few reclaimed phosphate pit areas open to the public, Tenoroc charges a nominal fee to fish. Its waters have produced exciting catches of bass for many, and they continue to produce.

Chapman and other fisheries biologists have been surveying these waters ever since the 6,000-acre site was donated by Borden Chemicals in 1982. Each year, they do electrofishing and then mark-and-recapture studies on several of the approximately 1,000 acres of mined pits and reclaimed lakes. They analyze their data and that provided by the anglers leaving the Reserve.

The popularity of old phosphate mines and the location's proximity to an urban area ensures lots of fishing pressure, about 100 hours per acre per year, according to the biologist. It is evident that even with restrictive measures, such as daily quotas on the number of fishermen, management regulations are essential to maintain a quality fishery.

Currently, on Lake B, a 16- to 22-inch slot limit exist. That means that bass between those two lengths must be returned to the water immediately. Additionally, only one of the four-bass bag limit can measure more than 22 inches. Such restrictions when enforced have kept the waters better than most waters in the state. A five-year study by the Commission was just completed, and it holds significant promise for the trend to continue.

Lakes A and C, each a little larger than 20 acres, are strictly catch-and-release waters, and both are recent "stars" in the Tenoroc program. The catch rates and size structure have improved substantially since the study began in January of 1984. Significant population expansion in both lakes, as the result of induced changes in the aquatic plant community, was facilitated by total protection of bass. On Lake A, catch rates have varied from a low of .57 to .74 bass per hour, and that's two to three times the average for most of

94

The author enjoys fishing deep-running crankbaits on the submerged humps and points in Tenoroc pits.

the state's public lakes. Bass catch rates on Lake C increased from .19 in 1984 to .60 in 1989.

CATCH AND RELEASE

"The catch-and-release regulation on Lake C produced highly positive benefits to fishermen," notes Chapman. "The resultant fishery is of exceptional quality. Observations made during the study parallel similar trends observed during the no-kill evaluation on Lake A. That further supports a case for total protection of bass in small, heavily fished waters!"

"As the bass fishing population continues to steadily grow in Florida, demands on limited bass resources will become even more intense," he says. "As a result, restrictive harvest regulations will, doubtless, play an important role in maintaining angler satisfaction. While other management alternatives are limited in application or inadvisable, recycling of bass through catch-and-release and other harvest restrictions may help perpetuate quality fishing."

It's unfortunate that some people still break our fishery laws and keep more than their limit. For those with such a penchant, Tenoroc, with its unique and varying restrictions, is not the place to go. There are motor restrictions on some lakes, including electric only on some and 10 hp limits on others. The "management by regulation" on Tenoroc waters is working, offering all anglers a better chance at catching bass. For those with deep-water angling expertise, it's a great opportunity to dredge up a giant bass.

Submerged trees in phosphate pits harbor heavyweight largemouth.

PITS GALORE

When you glance across 40 miles or so of Florida real estate containing thousands of miniature bass waters, you'll be dreaming of trophy-size largemouth. There are numerous pit fishing opportunities other than at Tenoroc. The formation of the pits south of Interstate Highway 4 occurred, for the most part, just 10 to 30 years ago as phosphate rock deposits were unearthed.

Today, some of the best fishing in this state is in the phosphate pits which lie chiefly in Polk County, between Orlando and Tampa. The area extends several miles south of the Interstate, and there are more. Phosphate pits also exist in Hillsborough, Manatee, Hardee and DeSoto counties to the south and west of Polk, and to a lesser extent, in the northern part of the state.

Channels, islands and variations of structure and depth are created as the massive dragline buckets dig through the sandy soil to get at the raw phosphate rock beneath. The depth of the newly created pits vary from site to site, but many run 40 feet or more.

The pits are all different in structure. Some lakes contain humps, deep holes and even "mountains" projecting above the typically-flat submerged landscape. Others have vast pad beds, cattails and bulrushes, and still others are nearly void of emergent vegetation. Many have sharp drop offs near some banks and some of the better ones even have a profuse growth of hydrilla.

The vegetation just off the deepest water is a good place to find pit bass. Better shorelines usually have the deep water nearby and structural characteristics that migrate along to the shallow feeding flats. Shad, golden shiners and tilapia abound in the pits and are the preferred forage for bass. Another popular treat for hungry

Bill Cork, of Plano, Illinois, caught his largest bass ever while fishing with guide Dave Hoy on a phosphate pit.

largemouth is, understandably, the crayfish. The numerous rock piles found in the pits hold substantial populations of them.

The smaller holes vary in clarity, depending on shoreline characteristics, drainage land and degree of water manipulation through the pits. The channels are deeper than those in our state's natural waters and provide pit bass the opportunity to migrate to and from deeper water.

Most knowledgeable pit fishermen can boast of never being skunked when spending a full day on the water. Catches often tally 15 to 20 largemouth, and releasing most fish is why pits remain productive. Studies by the Game and Fresh Water Fish Commission have revealed that the catch ratio in the state's pits is twice as high as the average for natural lakes. The pit fish will often average two and one-half pounds.

Anglers who fish pits regularly often catch 45 or 50 two-pound bass off a single structure. I have done that often and, of course, released them all. In fact, I've found that no other waters offer a better chance of catching, and releasing a limit.

The fishing in phosphate diggings comes and goes, so the successful angler should learn a dozen or more waters. Guides in the area have learned them, one pit at a time, by fishing them continuously over a period of several weeks. Most of them like to know of several man-made lakes where they can easily catch fish.

Public Pit Details

Any bait or tackle shop in Polk County can tell you of public access to hundreds of phosphate pits. The majority of waters lie within 30 miles of Lakeland, Information can also be obtained from bait shops in most of the small towns near pits such as Plant City, Mulberry, Haines City, Bartow, Auburndale and Winter Haven. The tackle shops can usually suggest public pits that currently provide good fishing. Many of them are unnamed, so specific directions are vital to finding the right ones.

It seems like each house in Lakeland has at least a john boat in the backyard that has spent most of its life on flooded phosphate grounds. And with a pit full of bass generally within half a mile of any residence, it is little wonder that locals can often be seen with watercraft in tow or atop their vehicle. For those bass chasers with a large bass boat, they must seek out one of the 10 percent or so of the pits that have ramps, or utilize a 4-wheel drive vehicle.

One good public fee pit is called the Saddle Creek Bass Club, located off Highway 33 on the northeast side of Lakeland near I-4. Horsepower restrictions, special days and many other regulations are in effect for this lake. I have caught many nice bass from it, and it is definitely worth a visit. For complete information before you go, call Don Roe at (813)644-2655. He'll send you the rules and provide instructions on how to find the secluded place.

For anglers wanting more information on the phosphate pits in this area of Florida, write to the Florida Phosphate Council, Box 5530, Lakeland, FL 33803. Regional information can be obtained from the Game and Fresh Water Fish Commission South Region. For guide service, contact Professional Bass Guide Service, P.O. Box 91663, Lakeland, FL 33804-1663 or phone (813) 858-0427.

For information on fishing at the Reserve, permit reservations or complete information on the regulations, write the Tenoroc State Reserve, 3829 Tenoroc Mine Road, Lakeland, FL 33805 or phone (813) 499-2422. While additional Tenoroc lakes are to be open in the future around a camping area, no accommodations currently exist at the Reserve. The nearest campground is the Yogi Bear Jellystone RV Resort Park (900 Old Combee Road in Lakeland, about 3 miles from the Tenoroc headquarters). About the same distance away is the Holiday Inn North on Socrum Loop Rd. (813) 858-1411.

Hotel reservations are recommended during the winter season for those planning a long trek to any of Polk County's pits. Accommodations are abundant throughout the Lakeland and Bartow areas and small towns in Polk County.

10

FISH-IN-THE-WATER

THE WIND WAS howling as we backed the boat down the short ramp at Uncle Joe's Fish Camp. White caps pounded the adjacent pier and breakwater. Fishing would be tough.

As we dropped our plastic worms overboard, finding a comfortable place to fish on Lake Weohyakapka during the gale was much more difficult than catching bass. A friend and I headed northeast toward the leeward shore of the shallow, flat lake, taking some spray over the side. Even that corner of the lake had small rollers that inhibited careful feel of our baits.

Our first isolated weed bed just off the perimeter vegetation produced a strike on my partner's second cast. He had flipped his plastic worm into the rushes about 15 feet from our boat and a big bass stopped the bait on his second lift. The fish boiled the surface in the four feet of water as he set the hook and missed.

The great largemouth bass action on Lake Walk-In-Water is often overlooked.

Three flips later, he again reared back, and this time a one-pound bass was swung from its watery environment into the boat in one quick sweep. My partner ducked and then reached for the bass, grasping it by its jaw. He released the small largemouth as I set the hook into its twin inhabiting the same rush bed just 20 feet away. The wind pinned us down, limiting our mobility, but we did take one more bass before moving to another isolated patch of rushes about 300 yards away.

The bass in the second patch were cooperative and we caught and released two more bass after missing two other strikes. A third and fourth bed of vegetation yielded similar results - some misses and some catches. Most of the largemouth were small and feisty, and some of those that escaped were tangled in the tall rushes before flipping off and dropping back to their environment.

Our largest bass, a three-pounder, was representative of the Lake Weohyakapka largemouth, long and healthy, but not overly fat. The lake's Indian name is not easy to pronounce and is better known as "Lake Walk-In-Water," "Lake Walk-In-The-Water" or "Lake Walking Waters." The clear waters produce lots of smaller bass, plus a few very large ones. Despite its track record of producing fish, however, it is an often-overlooked fishery.

Located about four miles south of Highway 60 between Lake Wales and Indian Lakes Estates, this 7,532-acre lake is the largest in Polk County and one of the clearest in the state. Walk-In-Water is shaped like a dish bowl and is typical of many natural lakes in the state. The spring-fed primitive lake attracts more than its share of wading birds and eagles. While Lake Walk-In-Water feeds into the Kissimmee chain of lakes (through Lake Rosalie) via the north-flowing Weohyakapka Creek, there are no lakes contributing to its water influx. Tiger Creek is near the southwest corner.

About 75 percent remains undeveloped, and no agriculture is present on Weohyakapka's shores. The latter fact makes for minimal chemical run off, which is unusual for many of the lakes in South Central Florida. Best of all, this is a fish-catchers lake. Under normal conditions, most anglers will catch bass.

SKUNKLESS FISHING

"Most every one of our tournament anglers catch bass here," says Craig Jolin, manager of Uncle Joe's Fish Camp. "Last month, we had 75 boats in the Pond Jumper Tournament here, and every fisherman caught bass. There were no skunks in the entire crowd."

The winner weighed in 14 pounds that day, and the largest bass was slightly less than five pounds. The following weekend, another tournament out of the county ramp down the road resulted in one angler weighing in 30 pounds of bass to top the field.

Don't get the idea that this lake is a big draw on the tournament circuit, however. It isn't. Eight or ten club tournaments a year are the norm, and down the road, Lake Kissimmee often sees that many on one weekend day. This lake, in fact, is not a big draw to any type angler. On an average weekend, only about 10 boats launch from the Uncle Joe Fish Camp facility!

When looking for an unpressured body of water with many more bass than fishermen, consider Lake Walk-In-Water. The fact that the lake is lightly fished is a gold mine for those wanting to avoid the oft-times congestion of the Kissimmee chain. Tossing a

Feisty, pier-bound Walk-In-The-Water bass are often fooled with a plastic worm.

black-grape plastic worm or tiny torpedo topwater plug will fool a bass or two about any time of the year, according to Jolin.

The lake produces lots of small and mid-size bass and a few giants. The largest bass taken one summer weighed 14 pounds, three ounces. Earlier the same spring, the monster might have pushed 17 pounds with pre-spawn body fat and roe.

Tactics, Lures & Bait

Most anglers who have fished the lake seem to catch bass. In fact, unless heavy winds completely blow away the fishing, you can catch fish from Lake Walk-In-Water almost all the time. The success of the average angler on the pretty lake is normally only limited by bad weather.

When winds are not a problem, the most productive bass pattern is flippin', especially when water is low. Get the bait back into the densest cover for maximum action. As I confirmed on a recent visit, fishing the isolated reed patches offshore is effective on the congregated fish there.

A slight wind will help drift the boat over the numerous offshore beds of "shrimp grass." A 1/4 or 1/2-ounce Rat-L-Trap or a 7-inch red shad worm rigged on a 4/0 worm hook below a 1/4 ounce bullet weight can be productive. Most submerged offshore grass patches lie just below the typically 3 to 4 foot visibility.

Fishing any offshore vegetation, whether emergent or submerged in the clear water lake, can be productive. Some of the better spots are where reeds are mixed with cattail patches. On the northeast side of the lake, there are several offshore reed patches. Mixed in with the reeds are hydrilla and underwater vegetation in some areas, ideal places to toss a Rat-L-Trap, topwater jerk-type bait like a Bang-O Lure or stick-type bait.

The fish on the lake are basically sight feeders because of the water clarity. The lighter-weight worm rigs, like the Carolina-rigged Weeny Worm, can be very productive also over the shrimp grass growing three or four inches off the bottom. Areas where the grass mixes with hydrilla or isolated reed patches are where the fish gang up. Largemouth relate to the lake's reeds year around. In the summer, fish them early in the day, and once the water temperature drops below 70 degrees, bass are in the reed beds all day long.

Walk-In-Water's canal system is also fairly productive. Some are very pretty, as well as fishy. Bass often move into the canals to spawn as the water warms up in the spring. Canals on the lake's east side run into Indian Lake Estates and some on the west side are just down from the public boat ramp. The latter canal system is fringed with old wooden seawalls which attract forage and bass.

To catch bass from the canals off the lake, fish them early with a topwater plug or shallow-running crankbait. Worms with light bullet weights are effective when flipped against the vegetation growing off the canal edges. The seawall structures along some of the canals are good locations to find bedding bass. The fish tend to want to bed up against something. The sand bottom over most of the lake does provide excellent spawning grounds.

When fishing shallow water in this very clear lake, it is wise to use a light line and make long casts to avoid spooking the fish. Monofilaments testing 8 to 12 are preferred by the regulars used to dealing with the clarity. Light lures are also in order to complete the balanced rig.

WALK IN THE SHALLOWS

The lake averages about four and 1/2 feet deep, but some waters are deeper. Some sections near the middle of the lake are

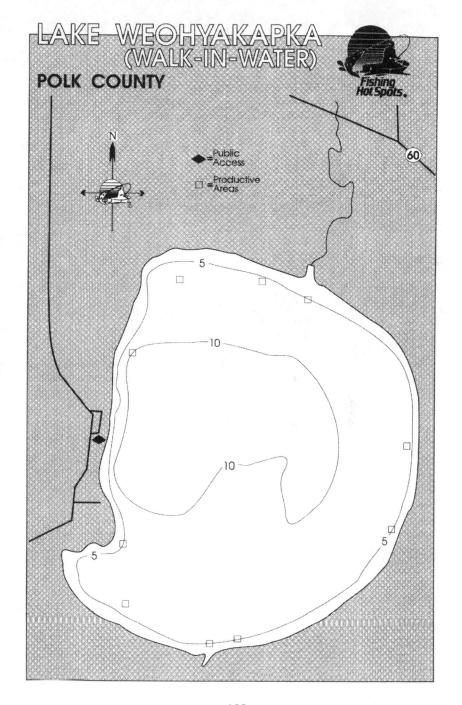

7 or 8 feet deep. During extremely low waters, it may be possible to literally walk right across the entire lake, which is probably why the Indians named the lake "Walk-In-Water."

Few wind blocks exist around the lake, so the waters are easily windblown. Because the lake is so shallow, whitecaps form frequently in the colder months when the weather is more unstable, and the lake can get very rough. Generally, though, in April the winds die off, and by summer, the wind is minimal. That's topwater time. Bass then will move to almost any topwater activity. In the morning, you can catch 10 or 12 fish before the sun gets very high.

After mid-morning, the bass often move deeper, or in normal water levels, tighter to the cover. In recent years, the lake level has been slowly receding, resulting in better fishing around the isolated reed patches. In fact, those on the south end have been consistently good. If the wind isn't blowing 25 mph, you can check them out.

When winds permit, boaters often catch small bass around the two fish attractors located in open water. Marker buoys define the submerged fishing structures. Other productive bass fishing spots on the lake include the dredge holes on the west side south of the public launching ramp. Sand was extracted from the lake to use in the construction of house foundations. In the winter, cold fronts will move bass to these deeper holes.

Dragging a plastic worm along the dropoffs during windy conditions can also be effective. Once you have located a drop of only a foot or even six inches, drag the worm with 1/4 ounce weight along the bottom. To slow the drift, try dragging a water parachute or 5-gallon bucket. I have used that tactic on the lake to take bass from the shrimp grass.

Letting the wind push you through an area is one of the best ways to fish Walk-In-Water. You can cover a large area on a drift and pick up a lot of largemouth offshore. If you drift through an area and get a bite or catch a fish, then throw out a marker and continue making passes. You'll need the marker to have something on which to line up the drifts.

Rat-L-Traps and diving crankbaits are both productive when employed over the submerged cover. Spinnerbaits and spoons are also effective on the lake. Fish a willow leaf blade spinnerbait in the bulrushes or a spoon with grub trailer for best results. On one day, a guide friend and a client caught and released over two dozen bass up to seven pounds on the artificials.

Another effective bait for the offshore areas is live shiners. In fact, if your target is a trophy bass, that should be your best bet.

The author caught this healthy Weohyakapka bass from emergent grass on a typically windy day.

Pull a golden shiner across an underwater grass bed or float one against a reed point and hang on to the rod.

RUNOFFS AND DOCKS

After heavy rains, the creeks and their mouths become contact points for bass congregations. When the water starts flowing in the two small creeks on opposite ends of the lake, the fish that have been scattered about the nearby vegetation will congregate at the mouths of those creeks. For an angler new to the lake, flowing creeks should provide a good start.

The great runoff fishing won't last long on the creeks. Often when the creeks are running, the bass are literally "stacked" on a sandbar at their mouth on one day. A day later, the bass have scattered and the previous patterns are no longer valid.

Docks, although limited on the lake, are good spots to try on bright sunny days. Crankbaits and worms are both effective in normal to high water conditions. While the dock fishing on Lake Walk-In-Water can be productive, many lake residents are very protective about the fishery around their property. Some feed the fish off their docks or back yards, and the majority are strongly opposed to abusing the valuable resource. Almost all practice catch and release. That's not a bad idea for visitors either.

STROLLING WILD SHINERS

Even pier-bound fishermen can get in on this lake's bass action. A very unique way to catch some big Florida largemouth from the lake is being practiced by a group of retired residents there who "stroll" after bass. Residents of Indian Lakes Country Club get their evening exercise with rod and reel in hand. The senior casters cast their Texas-rigged worms off the 10-feet tall pier and 'foot-troll' them along the pilings supporting the structure.

The community pier is shaped like a "T" and extends 1,200 feet toward deeper water. The top of the "T" is another 600 feet long and lies in six to eight feet of water. Each night during nice weather at least a dozen anglers walk every foot of it, almost 3/4 of a mile. The foot-trolling anglers reach around the occasional light post with their tackle and keep moving.

The anglers normally use light spinning tackle with 10-pound test monofilament. Handling big fish on light tackle can pose problems however. Bass often wrap line around pilings supporting the pier. Many huge fish have been lost, but a bunch of very respectable lunkers have not escaped. A 13-pound largemouth is the "foot-troll" record for this Lake Walk-In-Water pier.

LAKE DETAILS

Largemouth comprise 27 percent of the total fishery weight and 37 percent of the total fishery number, according to a March 1990 electrofishing survey by the Game and Fresh Water Fish Commission. The survey also showed plenty of bass forage including panfish, warmouth, spotted sunfish, brown bullhead, shad, shiners, killifish, silverside and other forage minnows.

Uncle Joe's Fish Camp, the only one on the lake, is located on the west shoreline just north of the county park. From U.S. Highway 27, take Highway 60 east for 8 miles. Then, turn south on Walk-In-Water Road and drive 5 miles to the camp on the left. Uncle Joe's offers a free launching ramp and other facilities, such as duplex apartments with heat, air conditioning and cable TV, RV sites with water and electric hook ups, restrooms, showers and benches to sit on and lie about the day's catch. A convenience store with food staples and bait is incorporated into the fish camp office. Guide service and trophy mounting can also be arranged.

For more information on Uncle Joe's, write them at 4335 Walk-In-Water Lake Rd., Lake Wales, FL 33853 or phone (813) 696-1101. For more information on the area, contact the Lake Wales Area Chamber of Commerce.

The county boat ramp is located about 1/2 mile south of Uncle Joe's off Lake Walk-In-Water Road. Turn east on Boat Landing Road to the excellent launch ramp. It provides access to the lake in all but the windiest conditions. During strong westerly winds, use caution when using this ramp. There is no place to dock or park the boat when the wind is pounding the concrete bulkhead.

11

HIGHLAND'S GREAT DISCOVERY

THE BEST FISHING in the state is probably the most overlooked. The highlands area of the state is located primarily in southern Polk County and, naturally, Highlands County. It is not near any major human population centers, but the largemouth populations are substantial!

On my first trip to Lake June-In-Winter, better known simply as Lake June, a friend and I caught about 20 largemouth that averaged four pounds each. We were shiner fishing submerged hydrilla beds on dropoffs in 10 to 15 feet of water. Several bass between five and seven pounds convinced me of the lake's productivity.

Lake June in the Winter and Istokpoga are just a couple of the great waters in the state's highland area.

We found the ledges about 300 yards off the southern shore across from the county ramp. From our anchored boat, we "tight-lined" seven to nine inch shiners on four rods. Action came quick and was steady throughout the overcast day. The summer afternoon showers culminated a great trip for both of us.

Lake June is a 3,504-acre of bass-laden water off Highway 27 at the town of Lake Placid. The lake is not typical of other super shallow dishpan lakes in the state. Instead, its depths vary considerably, and its shoreline is one of the most irregular. With average depths of about 10 feet, and some holes dropping to 20 or more, the lake offers the variety that most avid bass anglers enjoy when trying to establish several different productive patterns for catching fish.

There are about three dozen public launch ramps sprinkled around Highlands County. Some of the better ones are on Lake Istokpoga (northeast and southwest sides), the Kissimmee River, Lake Placid (northeast side), Lake Huntley (southwest side), Lake Clay (east and west sides), Lake June, Lake Francis (east side), Lake Sebring (southwest side) and Lake Jackson (Veterans Park). Good small-water ramps exist on both East and West Josephine Lakes, on Red Beach Lake, Dinner Lake, Little Red Water Lake, Lake Grenada, Lake Letta, Lake Lelia, Lake Lotela, Lake Pioneer and Arbuckle Creek. Lakes Grassy, Huntley, Jackson, Placid, Josephine, June and Istokpoga all have Commission-placed fish attractors which concentrate largemouth.

Lake Istokpoga Blossoms

The 27,692-acre Lake Istokpoga is perhaps the best bass fishing lake in South Florida. And that is a secret that many don't want spread around. Abundant vegetation helps keep the Highlands County lake reputation intact. The state's fifth largest body of water has been overlooked by anglers for years, while they trailered their rigs on to larger lakes, Okeechobee and Kissimmee. Only winter visitors in temporary residences "pressure" these waters.

Istokpoga, located a few miles southeast of Sebring off Highways 27 and 98, is 11 miles long and about seven miles wide. It remains fairly undeveloped due to being remote from big cities. The waters have abundant rushes, reeds and other emergent vegetation, and hydrilla and numerous submerged plant varieties.

Weed woes of the mid 1980's have been corrected. The hydrilla throughout the lake and cattails near shore were out of control in 1988, covering about 75 percent of the lake. The Department of Natural Resources treated the lake with aquatic weed killer and reduced the hydrilla to about 12 percent of surface acreage. That's manageable and forage intensive, ideal for a booming bass population, according to friend Tom Rosegger, fisheries biologist with the Game and Fresh Water Fish Commission.

Rosegger calls this lake, "Florida's best," and he knows first hand after extensive research and electrofishing for the Commission and after rod-and-reel angling from the bow of his bass boat. Recent fish population studies revealed that the bass fishery in Istokpoga is booming. In fact, the catch rate from creel surveys is about twice the state average, according to Rosegger.

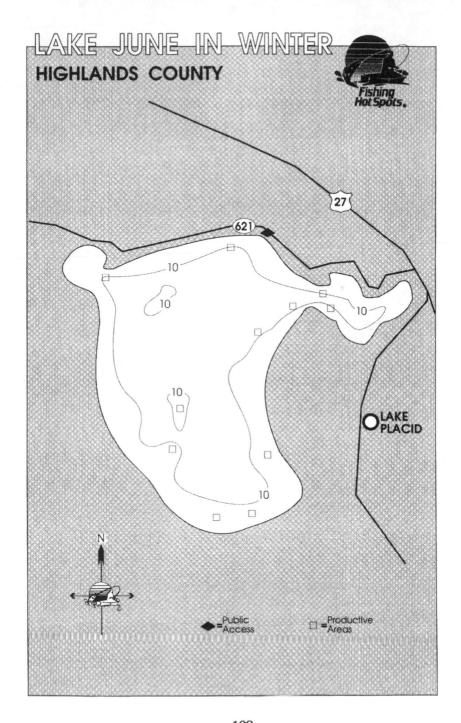

LAKE JUNE IN WINTER
HIGHLANDS COUNTY

Fishing
Hot Spots.

27

621

10

10

10

10

10

LAKE
PLACID

10

10

N

◆ = Public
     Access

☐ = Productive
     Areas

"Despite some low water levels and problematic aquatic vegetation, the lake's sport fishery is outstanding," says Rosegger. "A four-month creel survey generated success estimates of 0.52 bass per hour. However, the lake is one of the most overlooked in the state."

The studies indicated a surprising population of "quality" bass (over 15 inches) and "trophy" bass (over 22 inches). Almost a 400 percent increase in quality bass found during electrofishing was noted over a one year period. The trophy bass population in the huge, shallow saucer was 1200 percent more than 1989 figures. The lake record is around 15 pounds, but numerous bass over 10 pounds have been caught.

Many big bass have come from offshore waters. The northern, southern and eastern shoreline areas of the lake also produce big largemouth. Both trophy bass and smaller ones inhabit the emerging peppergrass beds on Istokpoga. Fishing the 10-foot deep channel can result in larger average size bass, however. Fish attractors also concentrate some largemouth.

There are two islands on the lake: Big Island on the east side and tiny Bumblebee Island (also called Little Island) in the southern portion. Both islands offer good deep-water vegetation and bass in them. Bumblebee has an eight foot ledge just off its shore, and it is a favorite honey hole of local bass guides. A few grass "islands" of emergent vegetation also exist in the lake.

The average depth in Istokpoga is around five feet, and the deepest holes are little more than 12. The southwest shoreline also has some quick drops. Scattered rock piles in Mossy Cove hold largemouth in the summer, if you can locate them. Two water-control structures maintain and adjust water levels in the lake, and two canals (the Istokpoga Canal and the C-41A Canal) allow runoff to the Kissimmee River and Lake Okeechobee. Istokpoga Creek on the east side, Josephine Creek and Arbuckle Creek, both on the northwest side of the lake are tributaries.

TACTICS, LURES & BAIT

Three pound largemouth are the average size of many catches today. Plastic worms rigged Texas-style and jig-and-eels pitched or flipped to dense cover both produce such fish. Berkley Power Worms in pumpkinseed and red shad colors seem to be very enticing to Istokpoga bass. Spinnerbaits with single blades are effective when fished over sparse vegetation and near the bottom

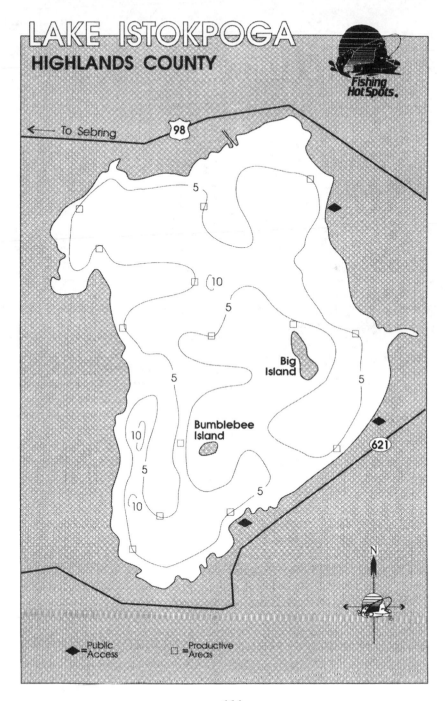

LAKE ISTOKPOGA
HIGHLANDS COUNTY

Fishing
Hot Spots.

← To Sebring   98

5

10

5

Big
Island

5

5

Bumblebee
Island

10

5

10

5

621

N

◆ =Public
Access   □ =Productive
Areas

The big bass of Highlands County are usually fat and healthy.

in five or six feet of water around weedlines. Blades that "tic" the plants draw strikes. So do spinnerbaits that helicopter down into the holes in the vegetation.

Most successful anglers fish the deeper masses of vegetation in six or seven feet of water. They stay away from the cattails and other super shallow-water growth. Sandy ridges with intermittent vegetation in the middle of the lake are highly productive in the spring months. The lake's canals and rushes on the sandy ridges hold spawning and post-spawn bass. Jerkbaits twitched on the surface are ideal for such places.

While weedless and topwater fare is the norm on this lake, vibrating plugs cranked down the boat lanes, over the tops of submerged vegetation and through open waters adjacent to the weedline, can be productive in the fall months. Shallow-running crankbaits worked along and over hydrilla beds are effective in the spring and winter months. Fronts affect the shallow lake in the winter, the fishing and water conditions.

The Indian name, Istokpoga, is pronounced "Iss-tock-POga" and translates loosely to "water where people have died." The big lake can rough up quickly with a strong wind, so the name is not surprising. Legend has it that several canoes of warriors were once swallowed up by these seas. Fishermen are well-advised to take care around approaching storms, fronts or on windy days. Lake levels are under the jurisdiction of the South Florida Water Management District, but not the white caps.

Numerous highlands lakes offer beautiful scenery and overlooked bass.

Several fish camps on the lake offer rental boats and cabins, and at least six launch ramps are available. The two public ramps have the most parking available. Numerous campgrounds are scattered about as well. Accommodations can also be found nearby in Sebring and Lake Placid.

While the fishing is great now, the nutrients (from spraying and other sources) in the lake are increasing at an alarming rate. Lake Istokpoga is currently undergoing restoration studies. Muck removal, revegetation and other components of a comprehensive plan for Istokpoga are under consideration.

The main tributary on Istokpoga is Arbuckle Creek, a 40-mile long cypress-lined runoff from Lake Arbuckle. The picturesque creek provides a good refuge from strong winds, but fishing pressure in it is heavy at times. Anglers fish the sunken trees of the banks and in the deep holes for good catches of bass. Boaters accessing the creek from the lake should be aware that a sandbar often exists at the mouth.

For more information on the Lake Istokpoga fishery, contact the southern regional office of the Game and Fresh Water Fish Commission.

CROOKED LAKE

Little known Crooked Lake is a crystal clear body of water that is often overlooked by bass enthusiasts. It has 23 miles of shoreline and averages about 15 feet in depth. Most people believe the lake to be shallow due to its marshy drainage basin that encompasses over 21,000 acres, but there are several deep spring holes over 30 feet. The official acreage is 5,538, but the current size is around 4,600 acres.

This lake, situated east of Highway 27 and south of Lake Wales, resembles what most of our South Florida lakes must have looked like before pollution and heavy shoreline development took its toll. You won't find muck-covered bottom and vegetation choking this waterway. The fairly infertile water is one of the region's most beautiful, isolated and scenic lakes.

For centuries, the only fishermen on Crooked Lake were the Tocobagas Indians. Archaeologists have reportedly found their canoes which predate Columbus' arrival. The Seminole Indians came later and had a village on the south side of this lake. They called the lake "Caloosa Lake." White settlers who displaced the Indians renamed it Crooked Lake for its irregular shoreline.

Wire grass near the shallow shores growing from clean, sandy bottom make this a good bass lake. Each year the clear, deep waters yield numerous largemouth over 10 pounds, and the reputed lake record is over 16. So, why doesn't the lake get its due recognition? It is off the beaten path, for one thing, and few Florida bassmen are comfortable fishing deep, clear waters.

To reach deep-water concentrations of largemouth offshore, dead-lining live shiners, trolling deep-running crankbaits or dragging Carolina-rigged plastic worms down the sandy drops work best on Crooked Lake. The almost "skunk-proof" fall-back plan of drifting a small worm along the depths works especially well in the summer months. In cooler weather, try the points and irregular bottom along the northern shoreline. Chunk spinnerbaits and vibrating plugs around the emergent vegetation on that shore during low light times.

A canal to Lake Clinch constructed around the turn of the century allows water to leave only when Crooked is very high. In the late 70s, the lake level dropped to record lows and has dropped further. Old docks are landlocked and navigation near shore requires care, but the lake remains ideal for recreation and esthetics.

12

FANTASTIC EASTERN CATCHES

MY INTRODUCTION to Farm 13 in the St. Johns River flood plain between Melbourne and Vero Beach was, to say the least, eventful. The first cold front of the year had just swept through, and guide friend John McKnight and I were bundled up as we motored along the "entry" canal. The temperature was hovering in the 40's, and we both knew that this day would be a test for the productivity of this fishery.

As expected the first hour was uneventful; we each caught a fish during the second, and about 10 a.m. the fishing got better. Within ten minutes we each had three strikes, landed two and released them. My six pounder about four casts later was an intended photo subject, so we took a break and shot several photos. I then slipped it back into the water.

Lake Blue Cypress, Fellsmere's Farm 13 reservoir and others around the Turnpike usually yield largemouth.

We began to shed clothing as bright bluebird skies finally generated some heat. The bass seem to realize that as well, and they turned on. We caught and released another dozen before our half-day venture was over. In fact, we had to leave while the largemouth were just beginning to feed on the surface.

Our average bass from the catch-and-release only lake weighed around three pounds. The 6,000-acre Farm 13 reservoir near Fellsmere in Indian River County is about the same size as nearby Lake Blue Cypress. Farm 13 seems to have abundant bass of that size, thanks to the release requirement. The reservoir (formerly a radish farm) was flooded only in 1987 and stocked with bass and bream in 1988. The Game and Fresh Water Fish Commission stocked 30,000 largemouth in the area after it was acquired by the St. Johns River Water Management District.

The early days of this impoundment found anglers easily getting their 10 bass (state limit at the time), and the Commission became concerned for the fishery. To prevent the fishermen from wiping out the entire bass population, the Commission passed the catch-and-release rule. While catch-and-release bass fishing can still sometimes be tremendous, crappie fishing in the cold months can be even better. Crappie were native to the network of irrigation canals on the farming operation. Crappie are important to Farm 13 because you can keep up to 50 of that species for the skillet!

Farm 13 consists of two large impounded pools, encompassing about 5 1/2 miles by 2 1/2 miles, and a canal that skirts them. The Stick Marsh, also called simply "Sticks" by local anglers, consists of about 2,000 acres of timber. It has a large area of flooded willows, wax myrtle and button bush throughout. The largest reservoir south of Sticks is an open-water reservoir with an average depth of six to seven feet. The canal runs south for 1 1/2 miles adjacent to the Stick Marsh, then runs west between the pools.

Fellsmere Farms, Inc., which owned the land, built three islands in the reservoir. They also made the cuts through the berms that existed when the impounded was constructed. That's important because the fish are able to migrate to the deeper canal waters during low water periods.

The existing "ramp" is suited for 4-wheel drive vehicles, and after a rain, you'll need another one to pull out your vehicle and the boat trailer. Small boats are best suited for this area, particularly if you want to pull and push the boat over the levee bisecting the fishing area. A cut through the main east-west levee is planned soon which will open up the southernmost reservoir to larger, heavier boats. Right now, parking is very limited along the Fellsmere Grade, a major flood-control levee that provides access. On weekends, forget about going.

An experimental stocking of red bass, or redfish as the saltwater gamefish is normally called, into Farm 13's freshwater was also performed by the Commission. Over 50,000 fingerlings were introduced into the only large, land-locked freshwater lake in the state that is salty enough for these fish to survive. In 1990, the lake received the red bass implant from the Department of Natural Resources Port Manatee Hatchery.

It should take a couple of years for the redfish to grow to catchable sizes in Farm 13 waters. Commission biologists believe

Farm 13 is a flooded bass area called "Sticks".

that the redfish will provide freshwater anglers with additional sportfishing opportunities. Regulations for the marine fish in Farm 13 will be the same as in saltwater - currently, one fish daily, 18-27 inch slot limit and season closed from March through May.

This is the first of three planned reservoirs which will, when completed, cover approximately 30,000 acres of Indian River and Brevard Counties. The other two won't be completed for a few years. For information on the Farm 13 fishery, contact Bob Eisenhauer, the biologist in charge of the project, at the Commission's Melbourne office, phone (407) 984-4876.

LAKE BLUE CYPRESS

Lake Blue Cypress is a beautiful example of a clean, cypress-studded natural lake. A written description does not do it justice. The lake is located five miles east of the Florida Turnpike (Yeehaw Junction exit) and 28 miles west of Vero Beach; turn north off Highway 60 onto Blue Cypress Lake Road and drive about five miles to the County Park and Middletons Fish Camp access points.

Land around the 6,555-acre lake is owned by the state, with the exception of the fish camp area on the west shore. The lake stretches about seven miles from north to south and is three miles wide. Most of the east side of the lake is marshland, and in fact, there's about 20,000 acres of marsh surrounding the lake. The lake averages eight feet and has a maximum depth of 14.

In the northeast corner is the lake's outflow: the 12-foot-deep "Big M" Canal, built in the 50's to deepen a natural drainage to the north. Running to the east is the ZigZag Canal, so named because

117

of its configuration. I've caught quite a few bass over the years from the canals which definitely run cold or red hot. The ZigZag Canal makes a sharp turn south and parallels the lake's entire east shoreline. It eventually turns east again and runs to Highway 512. A small creek feeds the lake from the southeast.

The shallow circular lake has many huge cypress trees on the north and west side, plus a few near the east bank. Sometimes called cypress knees, these roots project up above the surface of the water. Many on Blue Cypress are also hidden, depending on the water level, and they generally line the perimeter of the base of the tree. Fishing the cypress roots with a sinking worm can be difficult, but patience is the key to finding bass there.

Cypress trees can be found in all depths of the brownish-red stained water, but the ones in the deeper water generally house the most bass and a giant or two. The lake's isolated cypress trees farthest away from shore, in particular, can hold bass and they're usually larger than the bank runners near the trees.

The cypress trees on Blue Cypress are apparently fairly fragile and are very susceptible to lightning and strong winds. There is a lot of fallen timber on the east side of the lake, much of which is noticeable at the surface. Natural causes can pile up broken limbs and the upper torsos of weak trees on the bottom near the trunk.

There are also many bass-laden beds of lily pads on the west and south ends and a stretch of oft-times productive grass in two to four feet of water which runs the entire southeast side of Blue Cypress. There are four creek coves and two canals entering the lake on various sides which can also yield bass in the spring and fall months. Four fish attractors do their thing here as well. A fisherman can go wild eyeballing this lake.

The best months for catching one of the lake's giants is December through February, but greater numbers are usually caught later in the spring. Bass are caught year around in the areas of dense cypress trees, lily pads and grass, and most fishermen never venture away from these areas. But, in order to find large concentrations of big bass, you have to develop a productive pattern. The most effective pattern, generally, is to fish the small isolated pad areas which are several hundred yards out toward the center of the lake, rather than those huge beds close to shore.

Jerkbaits are a very effective lure for tossing around the cover on this lake. There's no hydrilla on this lake to worry about, so plugs with trebles can be retrieved in most open water areas. Fish the grassy shore on the eastern side in the spring also, and the deeper trees in the summer. Try worms in late summer and early fall, and check out the canals in the late fall. Many of the giants that I have seen caught on the lake came from the southwest shoreline area during the late winter months.

Another way to find bass is to check out the trees for signs of lizards. That's right, lizards. Guide friend Larry Lazoen was fishing Lake Blue Cypress once and noticed several chameleons on the numerous offshore cypress trees that speckle the lake. Many of the trees are several hundred yards from the swampy shoreline. The lizards were out moving about on the cypress knees, and every time they would get near the water, a bass would strike at it.

The angler would toss his top water bait toward that swirl and usually catch the fish. He and his partner caught six of the bass that they first saw strike at the chameleons playing on the cypress tree trunks. The four to six-inch long lizards must have swum out to the trees. That put them in a precarious situation.

The lake has gone through periods of rough times. In the 60's, it was one of the best lakes in the state. Heavy pressure from tournaments and, later, extreme low water due in part to nature's drought and in part to irrigation requirements of agricultural operations north and east of the lake, brought the lake to its knees (no pun intended). The lake level fell over six feet and the surrounding marsh dried up. The bass fishery suffered greatly.

As they say, "that was then." Today, the irrigation use is minimal, and the water is up into the marsh. The bassin' is back, the shad forage base is booming and the lunker largemouth are again bending fishing rods. In the past couple of years, about 30 ten-pound largemouth have been taken each spring.

The lake record is 18 pounds, 1 ounce and was reportedly caught by a woman on her first bass fishing trip. Many, many bass over 13 pounds have been caught in this relatively-unpublicized lake since. Just last year, Don Ferring of Boynton Beach caught a 16 pound, one ounce largemouth while fishing in a rental boat with his two daughters. He fooled the trophy with a live shiner fished near the cypress trees in the northwest corner of the lake. Add to such lunker bass possibilities the sunshine bass opportunities, and you have a great fishery.

THE REMOTE LAKE MARIAN

Some of my earliest big bass activity came from this remote lake, located east of Lake Kissimmee. Lake Marian is just two miles wide and about eight miles long, but it yields some heavyweight largemouth to those willing to travel past other "name" waters to get there. Numerous 10-pound-plus bass have been caught on the waters that I first fished in the early 70's.

I remember my very first trip fondly, when I caught an eight pounder from pads forming a point, and another trip in which I caught five bass over six pounds in one afternoon fishing the canals off the lake. There was another ten pounder and several over five that kept attracting me back to the lake. The fishing there today varies, but it is often very good.

The lake, located off Highways 441 and 523 near Kenansville, is primarily fished by "snow birds" from up north and by trailer home residents that call this oasis home. Marian can be reached by exiting the turnpike at Yeehaw Junction and then driving north about 15 miles. As you might expect, the 5,739-acre lake doesn't get a lot of outside pressure still. And that's good.

Marian is shallow with about 20 shoreline miles surrounded by sawgrass and cattle ranges. While not far from Lake Blue Cypress, this lake doesn't offer cypress-studded shallows. It does have a relatively clean bottom, except around the pad beds, numerous sandy shores and canals and some small, vegetated points that produce bass. You'll find a few holes of 20 feet, but most of the waters are less than 14. The average depth is around eight feet.

Mussel beds are prime spots for largemouth, but they are difficult to locate since they're frequently in open water away from shoreline structures. Winter and spring months are best for taking a big bass here. Fish the edge of the weedlines with Texas-rigged plastic worms. That's how I've caught most of my bass on this lake. Especially check out the points and pockets along the vegetation.

The weedline around four-mile point, and any emergent vegetation forming a point at the intersection of a small run-in on the south shore, can be prime spots for big bass. Use a Rat-L-Trap just off the vegetation for active fish that might be cruising the edges. A jerkbait twitched on the surface in the canals and on the grass edges early and late in the day, can also be very effective.

There are a couple of launch ramps on the lake, but facilities and accommodations here are not abundant. St. Cloud is 35 miles north for those who want to have complete services at night and commute a short distance to the lake during the day.

ALLIGATOR CHAIN OF LAKES

There are 26 lakes in the Upper Kissimmee Basin total more than 110,000 acres. They include the Alligator Chain which drains

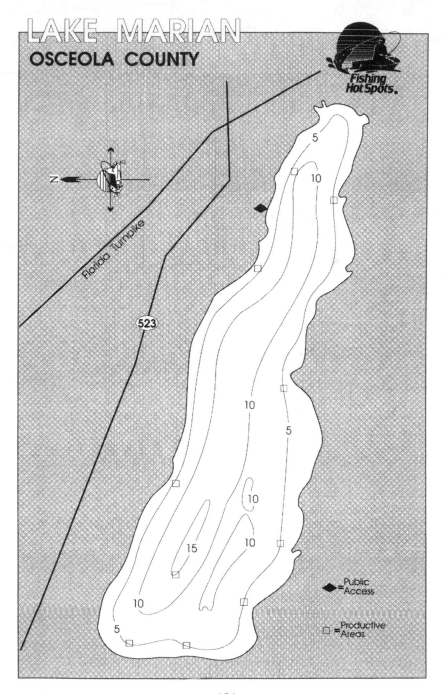

LAKE MARIAN
OSCEOLA COUNTY

Fishing Hot Spots.

Florida Turnpike

523

5

10

10

10

5

10

15

10

10

5

◆ = Public Access

□ = Productive Areas

through Lake Gentry's spillway into Lake Cypress. Brick Lake, Alligator Lake, Lake Lizzie, Coon Lake, Lake Center and Trout Lake are some of the better smaller lakes on the Chain that are accessible by boat. Cat Lake, Lake Conlin and Lake Preston flow into Lake Myrtle, and all these basin lakes have good bass fishing.

The Alligator Chain is located east of St. Cloud off Highway 192. Fishing pressure is minimal, due to the much larger "name" lakes nearby. This chain is picturesque, and in fact, was one of the first places that I ever did a photo shoot for an outdoor product manufacturer. These overlooked waters have lots of bass (photo subjects), and I have always caught some fish when on these waters.

Pretty Alligator Lake is shaped like a butterfly and is relatively clear and unpolluted. The north and south shorelines of the eastern "wing" are prime bass spots on this lake. The average depth is 12 feet, but deep holes scattered about the eastern half that drop to 35 feet hold some good largemouth during the winter and summer months.

My favorite spots are a deep-water dock on the west shore near the west outflow, the southeast point at the neck between the two "wings", the point just north of the small eastern most cove, and the irregular shoreline and point in the lake's northwest corner.

A couple of relatively poor ramps provide access to Alligator Lake. When the water level is low, launching is difficult unless you have a lightweight aluminum boat and 4-wheel drive vehicle. One ramp is unattended and the other charges a fee. There's another better launch ramp on Center Lake that provides (for a fee) access to the Chain.

Fish the 20-foot deep hole during the hot summer months and the southwest corner of Brick Lake the rest of the year. Other prime spots on the chain are the southeast corner of Center Lake, the northwest shore area on Lost Lake, the southwest and northwest shorelines of Lake Lizzie, and the drops adjacent to the north shore and southeast corner of Trout Lake. For maximum bass action, try also the grassy island in the north corner and the southeastern shoreline vegetation on Lake Myrtle, the relatively sharp drop off the west shoreline south of the canal outflow on Lake Preston, and the eastern shoreline on tiny Lake Joel (which is just south of Myrtle.

Tall emergent grass on the perimeter of the chain's lakes and sparse lily pads provide habitat for largemouth. Slash pine trees on the water's edge and black-clear water on many of the small lakes make this a delightful fishing experience. Relatively little

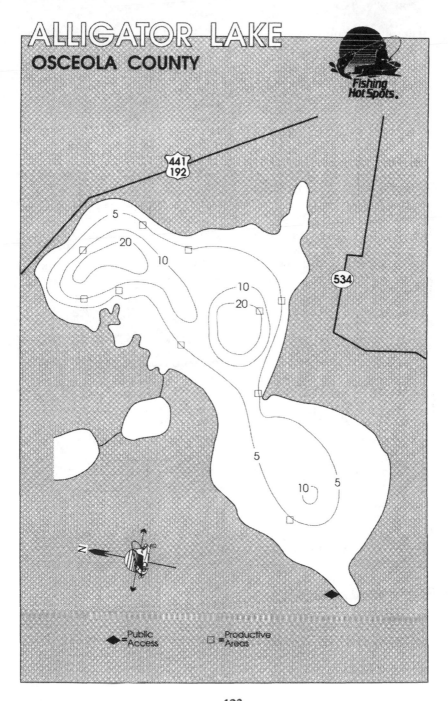

ALLIGATOR LAKE
OSCEOLA COUNTY

Fishing Hot Spots.

441 192

534

5
20
10
20
10
10
20
5
5
10

N

◆ = Public Access   □ = Productive Areas

development adds to the ambiance. Trophy bass can make the experience even better. A friend caught a 13 pound bass from tiny Brick Lake one day; it and Trout Lake are possibly the two best in terms of bass over five pounds.

The chain yields even bigger fish. Ed Cable caught a largemouth from the Alligator Chain in 1990 that weighed almost 14 1/2 pounds. It was the largest Florida entry in the Bassin' Magazine Big Bass World Championship and was worth more than $1,000. The St. Cloud angler caught the trophy on a live water snake.

The 148-acre Coon Lake has had a vegetation problem, but it is on the way to being solved. Its shallows were choked off by a band of 80-foot-wide floating plants, a barrier resulting from man's artificial manipulation of water levels in the chain. The dense bands of vegetation formed at low-pool levels and became uprooted from the bottom, which created floating tussocks. The floating "islands" of primarily dense pickerel weed and mat grass interfere with fish reproduction, according to Commission biologists. As a result, the biologists are currently using a barge weed harvester to remove them.

MERRITT ISLAND REFUGE

The Merritt Island National Wildlife Refuge, within eyesight of Kennedy Space Center, is remote largemouth bass fishing at its best. The refuge consists of impounded marshes and saltwater creeks and lagoons - most of which are brackish and generally shallow - about 45 miles east of Orlando. It's bounded on the east by the Atlantic Ocean and on the west by the Indian River.

The refuge is flat. Seldom are elevations found greater than 10 feet above mean sea level. The land is marshy with scrub vegetation, including saw palmetto, covering most of the dry areas. Cabbage palm, slash pine and oak grow on some of the higher ground.

Most of the refuge is open for fishing year round, although some areas are closed during waterfowl hunting season or space shots. A map with open areas marked can be obtained from the refuge manager and all Florida laws should be followed closely while fishing the refuge. Boats are usually permitted (except air boats) but small car toppers provide the most accessibility.

Many small ponds and sloughs exist on the refuge. Some can't be seen from either road or dike, and others have no approach by water, so you have to blaze a trail through the underbrush.

Wildlife of all kinds thrive on the Refuge. Over 2,000 alligators inhabit the area, in addition to raccoons, armadillos, bobcats, wild hogs, deer and, yes, snakes. The Merritt Island National Wildlife Refuge came into being in 1963. Its area now includes most of the 140,000 acres of land and water controlled by the space center. It's an overlooked bass spot, right on the Space Coast.

Nearby is a great fishing resort, called Jack Eckerd's The Great Outdoors. It's an RV/golf resort on Highway 50 just west of Titusville, but it has numerous lakes and ponds that are loaded with bass. Guests staying in their own RVs or in a park rental unit can fish the waters expertly managed for superb fishing. For information on The Great Outdoors, write them at 4505 Cheney Highway (SR-50), Titusville, FL 32780 or phone (800)621-2267.

St. Lucie River and Canal

The St. Lucie Canal, which connects the massive Lake Okeechobee to the St. Lucie River, offers excellent fishing beneath a series of spillways bordering it. The 38-mile long canal, started in the late 1800s, is part of the Okeechobee Waterway that offers cross-state navigation via river ditches from coast to coast. The St. Lucie Canal stretches from locks at Port Mayaca eastward to locks at Stuart. It is the most scenic of the South Florida canal waterways.

Erosion from the water movement and boat traffic has transformed the originally box-cut canal banks into much better fish habitat. Now, shoals and gradually sloping banks with profuse bulrush, maidencane grass and other emergent vegetation offer the angler a natural waterscape and the bass great habitat. Fallen pine and palm trees and an occasional rock outcropping add to the tremendous largemouth structure.

Grass shrimp and forage fish are abundant along the canal's expansive littoral zone. The gentle slopes of sand and rock make for good spawning areas and produce a better than normal canal fishery. Saltwater species, such as snook and tarpon, are sometimes a surprise catch in these waters on the east side of the "Big O."

The concrete spillways at the ends of irrigation canal networks offer a fresh water supply that brings food and oxygenation to the canal. Spillways, recessed into the canal banks, are not even head tall. Concentrations of feeding largemouth are attracted to such spots, so they should be focal points for bass fishermen.

Most spillways have pumps that allow water movement either way. They can fill the canal system or discharge water into the St. Lucie. The spillways are most active in the rainy season, and they always provide the best bass fishing when water is flowing into the

Worm manufacturer, Jack Doolittle, hoists a typical Farm 13 bass for a picture before releasing it.

St. Lucie Canal. Summer months are difficult to top, but largemouth can be taken year around on this canal.

The spillways can be fished from a boat, or they can be fished from the bank for those who want to drive along State Highway 76 which parallels the canal for much of its length. To find them along the road, simply stop at each bridge and check out the possibility of a spillway. Boat access is available at the county park west of Stuart off Highway 76 or at Port Mayaca near the intersection of Highways 76 and 441. For information on locking times, call the St. Lucie Lock and Dam at (813) 287-2665, and the Mayaca Lock at (813) 597-2339. Most of the better spillways around Indiantown are a long run from either launch/lock site.

Fishing the spillways more effectively is accomplished by boat. I'll fish the eddy water first, and then move in tighter on the water control structure to cast the faster water on the Okeechobee side of the outlet. Before moving on to the next spillway, I'll fish the quieter water on the Atlantic side of the outlet. Due to the current and normal water movement along the canal, a relatively-shallow bar is formed on the Atlantic side of the spillways. Bass are usually in one place or another.

Heavier, deep-running lures that get down quickly are best for the fast water. Other lures that don't sink fast are suitable for the slower runoffs. Anchoring or positioning the boat in the middle of the spillway and fan-casting the entire area is usually a good approach.

13

SOUTHWEST LAKES, CREEKS & CANALS

HOW CAN AN ANGLER have a quality experience while catching bass that may average only 12 or 13 inches in length? When he or she is catching them at over four times the average state-wide rate from beautiful, unique waters specifically designed for largemouth bass - that's the answer.

There are several ways to find such fishing near the Gulf Coast. One fish management area, called Webb Lake, was expressly designed for high yields and others, like the canal system throughout Charlotte County, just happen to be productive and overlooked.

Lake Trafford is another South Florida waterway that often produces bass.

Some of Southwest Florida's bass waters are custom designed - others aren't. Most provide quality fishing!

Webb Lake is located seven miles south of Punta Gorda. The waters there are unique in that they were custom designed by Game and Fresh Water Fish Commission biologists as quality largemouth bass habitat. The fishing has been better than expected, thanks in part to management regulations in place since its opening in July 1984.

Some of those include prohibiting the operation of gasoline motors, limiting usage to daylight only, requiring a Fishing License Stamp and a Wildlife Management Area stamp and totally restricting harvest. By imposing catch and release requirements for the first time ever in the state, the innovative program took a bold step. It had to.

Webb Lake's bottom consisted of infertile soils which, in turn, resulted in low productivity. A severe lack of prey and poor bass productivity meant the game fish needed protection. The fish that

127

are produced from these waters are slow growers and that's the reason for the catch and release regulation - to protect those fish.

Initially, the lake was only open for four days each week, but after determining that fishing pressure was minimal during the first two years, they opened it all seven days. Webb Lake had an initial population curve similar to other Florida waters when first opened. The bulk of the bass were 11 to 13 inches, but a few over 10 pounds also existed.

The first day the lake was open, at least one nine pound bass was caught and released, according to biologists working the Management Area. They have documented largemouth up to almost 11 pounds from the young lake since. Catches like that, though, don't happen every day.

The big brutes are even more rare now, according to Tom Champeau, fisheries biologist with the Commission. The immediate release of all largemouth bass caught in the lake is extremely important in maintaining the high catch rates. Non-compliance to the release regulation has occurred, he feels, with respect to the big fish during the first year. After that, bass mortality has been minimal and the system appears to be working.

The same numbers of largemouth are still present in Webb Lake, but the average size has decreased slightly. Although some of the larger bass were lost from the overall population in the last four years, Champeau is optimistic.

"The fishery has one of the highest catch rates of any water in the state," he says. "The anglers catch 1.3 bass per hour on Webb Lake and our norm throughout the state is about .3. The lake experiences relatively low fishing pressure and a high quality catch rate."

Today, the area is utilized by an average of two or three anglers each weekday and maybe 12 or 13 fishermen on a weekend day, according to Champeau. That includes bank fishermen and those from small boats. It is a low-use area today.

Low fishing pressure wasn't always the case, though, according to the biologist. When the lake first opened, like any new water, it received a lot of attention. They expected more than the 70 per day that showed up initially.

Regardless of the fact that a few bass may suffer hooking mortality, each angler will have a better chance of catching largemouth under the regulation. Without the catch and release program on Webb Lake, overharvest would occur.

The designer Webb Lake produces plenty of mid-size bass.

The waters attracted, and continued to do so, its share of anglers wishing to check out the unusual Florida habitat. Many of the visitors are from either Punta Gorda or Ft. Myers, which lie 20 miles to the south of the Fish Management Area. Some anglers come from Sarasota to fish the lake.

TACTICS, LURES & BAIT

Anglers with an ultralight spinning outfit can experience worlds of fun. One of my favorite rigs is a Berkley Series One B21 spinning rod with a small spinning reel spooled with 6 pound mono. An in-line spinner or an injured minnow plug, like a tiny Rapala, will catch numerous bass that may average only 12 inches, but will make up for their lack of size with spunk.

Bass can be caught most everywhere on the elongated lake, according to Champeau. Those anglers finding an area where the water flows into the lake from the marshes have a "gold mine" in front of them. The bass will be concentrated in such forage-intensive areas.

Plastic worms worked along the edges of the deep channel and over points are productive. Top water lures worked along the bulrushes, maidencane and other emergent vegetation are also successful, especially when deep water lies nearby. The extremely shallow areas don't normally hold a lot of bass.

Crankbaits are often effective around the cuts and points. When shoreline activity is non-existent, then locals opt for trolling down the channel with the electric motor. They'll tie on a small crankbait and work it right at the edge of the deep water. When it's hot on Webb, going to the deep water is an angler's best bet.

WATER CONDITIONS

The water is extremely clear in the summer, fall and winter months. During the spring, when the water is low and flow through the lake is negligible, an algae bloom will occur, decreasing visibility. Nutrients in the lake are then concentrated and the visibility is around four feet. When the summer rains start, pH levels drop as nutrients are flushed from the lake, and the bottom at 10 to 12 feet can be seen from the surface.

The fishing on Webb at any time of the year should appeal to all anglers interested in a fun outing on waters different than the typical natural lake. The transplanted Floridians from the north and tourists may be more familiar with the terrain of flatwoods islands which the lake offers.

Several unique concepts were utilized in developing the unique body of water located just east of I-75 at the Tuckers Grade exit in Charlotte County. The Cecil M. Webb Wildlife Management Area is a man-made, 350-acre lake with an enormous 16 miles of shoreline. In a state known for its natural, circular ponds and lakes, it's unique.

The area was initially a palmetto and slash pine thicket interrupted by numerous ponds that held water only seasonally. The ponds, with one or two exceptions, remained dry the majority of the year. Very few significant fisheries existed in the area prior to the development of Webb Lake.

Interagency meetings to design a lake that would offer good bass fishing while allowing the excavation and removal of borrow material came off well. Over three million cubic yards of fill were removed in a well-thought-out manner. The DOT cooperated fully with the Commission recommendations regarding the areas and slope of the excavation work.

DESIGN FEATURES

The lake has a varying bottom contour and a wide range of depths. Although the lake is only one and one half miles in length, a series of lagoons extend laterally from the main channel. That accounts for the extensive shoreline area. The lake was designed with future management program implementation in mind. It has three distinct bodies of water connected by two narrow necks. That feature allows the separate lake segments to be isolated if need be.

The Webb Lake lagoons on the east shore are designed to be shallow to encourage vegetation growth and increase production areas. The main channel that runs the length of the impoundment is approximately 30 feet wide. The channel depth is ten feet, deep enough for maintaining a fishery during any extreme low water drought that may occur in the future. Rain is extremely important to this fishery. The main tool in producing a good fishery on Webb Lake is the flooding of adjacent marshes. During summertime, a lot of rain floods the marsh. The drainage basin is just over 20,000 acres, an extremely large drainage.

The shallow, vegetated habitats produce a lot of forage fish, such as bluefin killifish, coastal shiners, and other important food fish. The marshes drain into the lake, so there's a constant wash of forage to the bass population in the lake during the summer. By winter, the food is mostly gone, but the bass have fattened up during the summer and fall.

FISHERMAN ACCESS AND LAKE DETAILS

The western shore and lagoons along it are designed to permit bank fishing. Unlike the shallow, highly-vegetated eastern shoreline, the western bank is constructed with a steeper slope so that only a thin margin of aquatic plant life has developed. The bank slopes extend out to between four and six feet in depth before becoming totally irregular.

Wade fishermen are pretty much confined to the shallow lagoons. In deeper waters, boulders, stumps and rock formations were left intact or positioned in desirable areas to provide "bottom relief," as the biologists refer to structure. Such habitat concentrates the largemouth bass in the lake.

Boat ramps placed near the ends of the long lake and one near the middle provide excellent access for boaters. A road extended along the length of the lake's western shoreline allows access to the ramps and to those wishing to fish the areas specifically designed for bank fishermen.

An angler with a bass boat can use the rig but may not use the outboard (gasoline) motor. He'll have to rely on his electric motor to get around the lake. Oars or paddles for other craft are also options. Due to the long, thin shape, boaters can easily get out of the wind in several areas.

A dam on the north end of the lake controls outflow into the south prong of Alligator Creek and also acts as a barrier designed to contain fish. With that, the capability also exists to fluctuate Webb Lake water levels for management purposes.

For a map and brochure on the Webb Lake Fish Management Area, write to the Game and Fresh Water Fish Commission, South Region Office. They can provide additional information on the unique fishery at Webb.

CHARLOTTE'S OVERLOOKED CANALS

Neglected waters usually offer some of the best bass fishing in the state, as I've found out while fishing canals near Port Charlotte. Overlooked canals in Southwest Florida are just waiting to be explored, and most provide great bassin'. Drive down any major highway or rural road in this part of the state, and you're bound to parallel a canal.

South Florida's entire system of fresh water channels are a great opportunity to find bass, lots of them. I have fished the canals with Larry Lazoen who has guided on those canals for many years. The Port Charlotte resident fishes 25 miles of canals that are open in the Gardens of South Cove area. That's 50 miles of shoreline where largemouth of all sizes are numerous.

When searching for optimal fishing waters, Lazoen prefers canals that aren't heavily populated. Canals in the country, with heavy shoreline cover such as pencil reeds, cattails and bulrushes are ideal fishing spots. Some canals, however, get completely choked over with hyacinths, and that kills the fishing for a while. The better ones are those that stay open year round.

It is wise to observe the canals from season to season to determine the better ones. Most canals range from 10 to 12 feet deep, with an average depth of six feet. The better ones are at least three feet deep. Some will be silted, especially at those points where a little finger canal enters a larger body. If the water has any kind of flow at all and is clear, then the fishing will be good. Most of the better canal waters in southwest Florida are normally dark, tea-colored, but if you can see the foot of your trolling motor, you're in business.

Clear water canals with visibility up to five feet are also excellent producers of fish, but the catching is tougher for the average fisherman. Long casts with topwater plugs early and late in the day are often required for success.

The canals of Southwest Florida offer seclusion . . . and bass.

There are a lot of bass in the three to five pound range in the canals, because many have been in existence for at least 25 years; they are mature enough for huge fish.

TACTICS, LURES & BAIT

In April, May and June, before the rainy season arrives, those canals that are choked with hyacinths won't be as good as the others for artificial-lure tossers. Shiner fishermen, however, have a prime bass spot to try out. When hyacinths start to raft up, shiner fishing under the floating cover will produce big fish. Many shiner fishermen catch bass up to 14 pounds in the waterways.

The key is finding those South Florida canals that don't get choked with hyacinths. If they get choked over, everything under them dies; the other grasses and vegetation disappear. Then, when the rains come and flush it out, it takes a while for the bass to get back in and rejuvenate the canal. Almost every canal will have some kind of vegetation, however, and that keeps the pH levels optimum for successful angling. Too low of a pH, due to little or no vegetation, is cause for concern. Fish will move elsewhere.

Top water lures may be the best overall bait choice to attract bass. A two-inch chrome plug that matches the small size of the bass forage found in these waters is preferred by many local anglers.

133

The waterways just don't contain forage in large amounts or size. A shiner population is present, but neither threadfin nor gizzard shad are available in most canals. The primary prey fish there are tiny guppy and molly-type minnows. The minnow-foraging bass are fooled by small topwater plugs that closely resemble the baitfish.

Lazoen will throw the small plugs on 12-pound Trilene XL, and in canals with heavy cover, he'll toss spoons or buzz baits on 17 and 20-pound test. Plastic worm fare offered usually warrants 14-pound monofilament.

One of the most accessible and productive waterways is the Nine-Mile Canal near Port Charlotte. Right in the middle of town are miles of canals that receive virtually no fishing pressure. One such canal, called Morningstar Waterway, is an excellent place to catch fish. There are lots of houses and docks right on the canal, yet, like many other canals, it's an overlooked waterway.

LAKE TRAFFORD

Just three miles west of the farming community Immokalee on Highway 890 is the forgotten Lake Trafford. The 1,494-acre southwest Florida lake off Highway 29 has had its share of aquatic weed problems through the years, but it continues to provide good bass fishing to those that know the secrets of Trafford.

The lake with drainage from the Corkscrew Swamp, has a spotty history. It was one of the best lakes in the country back in the 40's with numerous 10 pounders caught daily. Then, it fell on hard times. The lake is extremely shallow with a maximum depth of only 10 feet and surrounded by a farming community with excessive nutrient runoffs, so aquatic vegetation, particularly non-native types, have their way with this body of water. In the 50's, the Collier County lake was dominated by rough fish, poisoned in 1962 by the Commission, and restocked. It reopened in 1964.

While the stocking was successful, the old reputation persisted. Today, those anglers tossing weedless lures in waters that average four to eight feet often catch several largemouth in a morning. Fishing pressure, however, is minimal, and that's good for those that chase trophy bass in the lake's masses of vegetation. While the lake record is just under 14 pounds, plenty of 10-pound plus bass swim in these waters. The profuse vegetation doesn't lend itself to yielding the trophies easily.

A public ramp provides access to the sawgrass saucer of a lake. Trafford is only four miles long and about two miles wide, so it is easy to cover by bass boat in a day's fishing.

14

THE GULF'S RIVER BASS

THE SMALL LARGEMOUTH that cleared the surface froth was a welcome addition to our day's tally. Guide Bill Pickhardt and I were fishing one of my favorite spots below the Shell Creek Reservoir on a Peace River tributary. We had released about seven largemouth and three high-flying snook from the foamy water that morning. The action was indicative of the fun that lies just five miles east of Shell Creek's confluence with the Peace River.

Southwest Florida's Peace River has abundant freshwater bass, but due to its reputation of having pollution problems near the headwaters, that fishery is often overlooked by local anglers. The Peace River tributaries near its confluence with the upper reaches of Charlotte Harbor are well known for their tarpon, redfish and snook. The river originates from Lake Hancock near Bartow and flows south to Punta Gorda; it has over 500 shoreline miles in the watershed, and most of them are freshwater. Waters close to the harbor may be brackish, but the bass don't mind.

Feisty largemouth in the Peace and other rivers of South Florida provide thrills to anglers in the know!

On my first visit to the area several years ago, Pickhardt and I covered the Peace and its tributaries in his aluminum boat. We fished the fast water just below the dam and caught six largemouth bass in a just over one hour. We had additional action below the Punta Gorda water supply reservoir. Four junior-sized snook fell for our bass offerings and displayed their high-jump abilities.

The highly phosphate-enriched water pouring over the dam beats the water to a froth, and suds cover the surface. Fish don't seem to mind the foam canopy overhead, though. I've taken up to a dozen largemouth averaging two pounds each from the spot.

Tactics, Lures & Bait

Several artificial baits are effective in the Peace River. Jointed-minnow plugs, crankbaits in silver with orange hues and vibrating plugs that resemble shad are great lures to toss in the moderately stained waters. White and brown jigs with optional color-coordinated trailers are also productive.

Casting is generally more productive than trolling, with one hour before to one hour after a tide, being prime time to catch the bass. Live bait enthusiasts opt for native 5-inch long shiners. They'll place a float about 36 inches above the lively baitfish and will catch plenty of largemouth.

The prime areas to fish either type of bait are the backwaters off creek channels. The big bass lay deep in the flowage just out of the fast water in eddies and wait for forage to pass. Excellent bass fishing for both quantity and quality fish exists on Shell Creek downstream of the dam. Similar action can be found on Myrtle Creek which runs parallel to Shell Creek and dumps into the Peace just below the point where Shell Creek does. Catches of 15 to 20 bass by two anglers on both tributaries are not uncommon. They may average two pounds, but not all area largemouth are small.

Shell Creek and Prairie Creek, the tributaries above Shell Creek Reservoir, are both excellent bass waters. Prairie has produced at least one 12 pound largemouth, and a Miamian caught a 14 pound, 15 ounce lunker on a silver and black broken-back Rebel from Shell Creek a few years ago.

Where To Look

Bass over 11 pounds have been caught from the Peace River and its tributaries. Larger fish seem most accessible after rains when the creeks are flowing high and fast. Once floods fill the banks of the Peace River watershed and overflow, however, fishing suffers. Water levels above normal readings result in some residential flooding and shut off the fishing for a couple of weeks.

During moderate rainfall, water in the Peace River basin is predominately fresh. Floating water plants become numerous and even clog some tributary passages. Water hyacinths provide forage, such as freshwater shrimp and other food organisms. The plants float down the watershed until the Gulf's high salinity content terminates their existence.

Bush and tree-lined shores are common on many of Peace River tributaries. Reeds, cypress and palm trees co-exist with

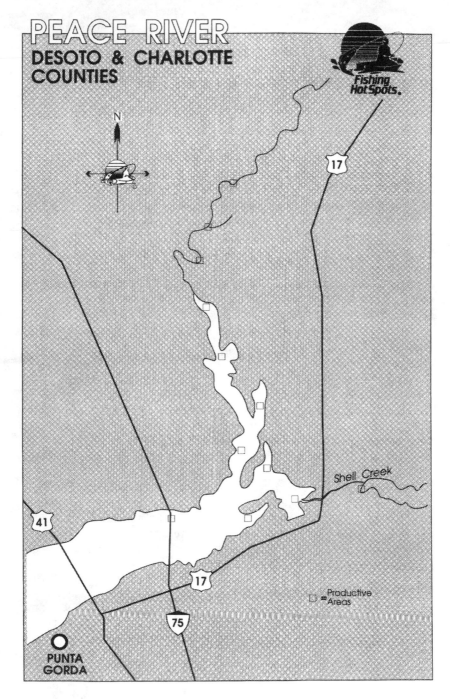

PEACE RIVER
DESOTO & CHARLOTTE
COUNTIES

Fishing
Hot Spots.

N

17

Shell Creek

41

17

75

□ = Productive
Areas

PUNTA
GORDA

submerged brush and scattered mangrove trees, and offer all largemouth great habitat. Quiet, beautiful waterways flow gently downstream through deep water bends and shallow coves shaded by numerous lily pads. Overhanging canopies of trees add to the scenic beauty of this environment.

Small bass are common in the upper reaches of the Peace River, including Gunter Creek and Deep Creek. I explored those waters on another trip and found very cooperative bass. Bayous and sloughs off their main channels should continue to be productive overlooked spots along the two waterways. On one of Pickhardt's guide trips to Deep Creek, 33 bass were caught and most released. Their four 'keepers' each weighed over 5 pounds.

The two anglers also caught and released several snook in Deep Creek that day. Snook are difficult to separate from largemouth bass, since they also inhabit shoreline cover. Bass lures thrown nearby naturally attract the brackish water fish. Bass anglers have caught snook weighing over 30 pounds while casting small, injured-minnow plugs. Both bass and snook in the Peace river tributaries often frequent the eddies. Such places where tide or current can't make up their minds are usually forage-intensive.

RIVER DETAILS

The Peace River meanders some 120 miles through four counties, and is one of the state's longest rivers. It has a drainage area of 2,350 square miles. Unlike most south Florida rivers, deepened and straightened by channeling and flanked by development, it has remained almost entirely as it was over 100 years ago. The Seminole Indians called it the Talakchopko, and the Spanish tagged it El Rio de La Paz (meaning River of Peace).

"Although still scenic and beautiful for the fishermen and canoeists who visit the river each year, it is being seriously mistreated," says Fisheries Biologist Tom Champeau, of the Game and Fresh Water Fish Commission. "The upper reaches, the first 14 miles south of Lake Hancock, are the most seriously and continuously disturbed parts of the river."

"In the upper sections, the natural diversity of fish populations has, however, been displaced by gar, mudfish and the exotic blue tilapia," he continues. "Such species thrive in polluted waters and are an excellent indicator of degraded aquatic habitat."

Municipal and industrial pollution of Lake Hancock, the river's headwater, and agricultural discharges within the river's flood

138

Many of the rivers in this area of Florida produce small bass like this one.

plain, have altered the aquatic ecosystem. However, pollution on the river's source have been slowed. In 1987, the city of Lakeland, a major source of effluent, stopped dumping into Banana Lake, which in turn empties into Lake Hancock.

Phosphate was first commercially mined in the state at the Peace River in 1883, and a few years later, several mining companies were dredging ore from the river. In the late 1800s, steamboats even made their way upstream to almost Fort Meade. Nature has since turned the evidence of such turmoil into oblivion.

As one travels the upper river in Polk County today, clean tributaries to fish are easy to identify, according to Champeau. There is often a distinct line that forms where tannic-stained water from the tributaries meet the cloudy green brownish color of the polluted main river. Further downstream, there are no lines and little pollution, just overlooked bass.

Ramps are scattered along the river; one at Pioneer Park in Zolfo Springs on Highway 64 and the Gardner public ramp 24 miles downstream just below the Charlie Apopka Creek tributary, are ideal for smaller craft. The Peace River is part of an official canoe trail, and canoe outfitters are located in Arcadia.

OTHER FLOWAGE OPPORTUNITIES

The Manatee River is 60 miles long and has a drainage area of almost 350 square miles. A dam prevents saltwater intrusion and the upper reaches are affected by agricultural runoff. Bass fishing is spotty in the low to middle portion where banks are heavily developed. Some largemouth are caught by locals or wise visitors that can quickly develop a productive pattern.

The Myakka River is about eight miles longer that the Manatee, and its drainage area is only about 235 square miles. Its water quality is very good, and the bass fishing, in general, is much better than that found in the Manatee. Pastures in the upper section contribute to bacteria, but most of the pollution problems are in tributaries flowing into the Myakka.

The 29,000-acre Myakka River State Park, 18 miles southeast of Sarasota on Highway 72, has a couple of lakes that shouldn't be overlooked. The Upper Myakka Lake is 1,020 acres and the Lower Myakka Lake is 640 unspoiled acres in the park's Wilderness Preserve. The upper lake is reportedly the largest purely rain-fed body of freshwater in the state. The depth in the upper lake varies from about three feet in the dry winter months to six or seven in the summer rainy season. A dam separates the lake from the river.

Myakka is the largest and most primitive of the state's 125 state parks, so it is normally less crowded than the others. Canoe rentals on the Upper Myakka Lake, camping, cabins and other facilities make this an attractive spot to visit. Check the park for hours of daily operation. There is a small admission fee.

While there is no such place as Skillet Creek, there is a Fisheating Creek that generates the same thoughts. Camping and fishing are the enjoyable pastimes on Fisheating Creek, not necessarily the eating of fish. The creek is located on the west side of Lake Okeechobee south of Palmdale off Highway 27.

Fisheating Creek is small, about 50 feet wide, over most of its course through its natural drainage basin, the only natural one that the Big O has, in fact. Cypress-lined banks twist and turn through wetlands, heavy underbrush and oak hammocks.

In the dry season, much of the creek is just that, dry. Only small potholes exist, but they usually hold small bass. The dark waters move slowly, even in the rainy season, and splits into two streams time and time again. Canoes are the best way to explore most of these areas. Access to all Fisheating Creek is not certain.

CALOOSAHATCHEE RIVER OPTION

Lake Okeechobee and its tributaries and outflows are known for bass, yet one of its freshwater outlets has some surprising fishing for giant "large-mouthed" sport fish that run up to 20 pounds. Some of Florida's finest snook fishing is taking place right

The Peace River yields more big largemouth than many anglers realize.

beside largemouth bass action on the black water Caloosahatchee River, just west of the Big O's Moore Haven Lock.

A few guides out of Roland Martin's Lakeside Marina at Clewiston have been getting in on the Caloosahatchee River combo largemouth and snook action for some time. Bert Fischer has left the lake action on numerous days to cash in on the little-known river fishing. On one of his better treks to the river, the guide and a client caught and released several largemouth and 14 big snook which ranged in size from 5 to 15 pounds.

The Caloosahatchee, which means "River of the Calusa Indians," is actually classified as a canal, because of its three locks. It traverses Hendry, Glades and Lee Counties, and four cities: Cape Coral, Fort Myers, La Belle and Moore Haven. The river stretches more than 75 miles from the heartland of South Florida and contributes more than 70 billion gallons of water to irrigate inland citrus groves, sugar cane fields, farm lands and pastures.

The westward-flowing river is controlled by the South Florida Water Management District and the U.S. Army Corps of Engineers. Moss-draped oaks and lush under growth dress its banks as the river reaches La Belle at mile marker 30.

April and May are the two best "open season" months on the Caloosahatchee and noon to dark offers the best time, according to Fischer. It was late afternoon when he caught his largest snook, an

141

18 1/2 pounder. The snook season is normally closed June through August, but the catch and release fishing then is tops, and so is that for river largemouth.

Fischer suggests fishing the cuts from the Moore Haven Lock westward to the Ortona Lock (at mile marker 20.9) near Ft. Myers. Downstream points are usually the most productive. If locking through, allow about 15 minutes per lock with no delays. While the locks are open most daylight hours, it's wise to check with the Corps in Clewiston at (813) 983-8101 or call the locks on the waterway directly: Moore Haven Lock (813) 946-0414; Ortona Lock (813) 675-0616; Franklin Lock and Dam (813) 694-2583. Public facilities are at the Alva Access area, approximately 1/2 mile east of the bridge, at La Belle Lions Club Park, 1/2 mile west of Highway 78, and at Barron Park, east of Highway 29 in La Belle.

Snook have been caught right alongside largemouth on topwater plugs all the way to the Sanibel Causeway. For more information, contact Fischer at 249 Tropical Village, Clewiston, FL 33440 or (813) 983-8902

Sunshine Alternative

Sunshine bass in the Peace River provide a fishery that most South Florida anglers seldom see. The fish love cold weather, and they can certainly heat up an angler's day. The sunshine is a sterile cross between the striped bass and the white bass and must be stocked. They grow fast and they fight hard, two qualities that make fishery managers and fishermen happy.

The Peace River near Charlotte Harbor is an interesting area that hybrid striped bass fishermen may want to check out. Fingerlings, one to two inches long, have been stocked, along with larger sunshines ranging from 12 to 17 inches. Many individuals are four pounds, their maximum weight in these Florida waters.

Sunshines in the river inhabit bridges, sand bars and deep holes in the area. They will hit any artificial lure resembling a shad. Tail spinners, in-line spinners, spoons, crank baits, vibrating plugs, jigs and plastic grubs can be extremely seductive to the hard-hitting sunshines. Naturally, live shad and minnows are productive for bait fishermen. They will also strike grass shrimp

Water temperatures in the low 60's are conducive to catching one of Peace River's hybrids. The cold weather slows down forage fish which results in a great opportunity for the roving schools of sunshine bass. They'll continue to hit well until the spring waters begin to warm.

15

ST. JOHNS SHALLOW PASTURES

THE LIGHTNING CRACKED and rain pelted us when we crossed the lake. It got worse just as my partner and I glided into a boat stall at the marina. The boat had run out of gas!

Such things only seem to happen to me when I am fishing with friend Wayne Graham. We had to stand in the pouring rain to crank his boat onto the drive-on trailer that day. The Titusville angler and I did have a successful venture to Lake Winder, fortunately, before the rains.

We caught and released several schooling bass on vibrating baits and worms that hot July afternoon. The schoolers surfaced about 5 p.m. and preceded the showers by 45 minutes. In that brief period, we caught 15 or so, and then had to make an 8-mile beeline run for Poinsett Lodge to outrun the mean thunderstorm. We hated to leave the red-hot action, but we had no choice.

The St. Johns River from its headwaters north to Puzzle Lake is the least fished stretch of this big bass producer.

Wet summer afternoons are common on the St. Johns floodplain in the summer, but droughts seem to occur every three or four years. The river flowing through Lake Washington often disappears during dry periods. So does Lakes Hellen Blazes and Sawgrass near the headwaters of the river. Those stretches of the river, however, produce excellent bass fishing even though they are extremely shallow most of the year.

I often fished that portion of the river when I lived in Melbourne and Palm Bay years ago, and since, I've been back many times, often with guide friend Bob Stonewater. We have worked much of the stretch south of Puzzle Lake. On one outing, I caught and released a couple of largemouth that were bragging size. They totaled 18 pounds and came from the river near Lake Winder.

The productive spots on the upper river are similar in nature and geography. While this north-flowing waterway is up to 3 miles wide near its confluence with the Atlantic Ocean near Jacksonville, the pasture-bound headwaters 180 miles away south of Melbourne can, at times, be jumped across during a drought.

The bewildering maze of channels twists through treeless grasslands. Tannic acid-stained waters flow through palmetto hammocks and sawgrass bogs that dot the tropical plain. The meandering stream contains overlooked largemouth fishing that I've known about since the early 70's. Lakes Hellen Blazes, Washington, Winder, Sawgrass and Poinsett interrupt the river but not the fishing. Year round, bass are caught in its natural lakes and in the unique narrow and twisting river, where both banks can be cast from the same spot.

Largemouth up to about 14 pounds are taken from the varying river depths. In fact, hundreds of bass over 10 pounds have been taken from the lonely stretches of river between Puzzle Lake and Lake Hellen Blazes. The fishing pressure along the primitive water course is minimal, although Melbourne, Cocoa, Titusville and Orlando are just a short drive away.

Downstream From Lake Poinsett

Just north of heavily traveled highway 50 lies Lake Cane on the west channel of the St. Johns. Lake Cane offers lily pads in three to four feet of water during high water levels. The east channel flows through small Lakes Ruth and Clark, where fishing is excellent in the sloughs and cuts along river stretches and in the tiny lakes. The river comes back into one channel between highway 50 and Florida state highway 520 near Half-Way Lake.

The river between there and Lake Poinsett, west of Cocoa, offers numerous bass among reeds and bulrushes that often crowd the bank. Most vegetation grows in four feet of water and less. The river's bass fishing can be extremely hot or cold, depending upon the water level.

In this section of the river, fish the bulrush and reed points in two to three feet of water for largemouth bass. Also, lily pads off the main channel are great spots for trophy largemouth. The mouth of the sloughs off the river channel often yield schooling

144

Guide Bob Stonewater can usually find heavyweight bass on the Upper St. Johns.

largemouth in the spring and summer, and trophy bass during the wetter early summer days when water levels are higher than normal. The outer bends of the river also offer excellent largemouth fishing when depths are 3 to 10 feet. Locate shoreline vegetation adjacent to a dropoff or deep hole on the outer bend of the river.

LAKES POINSETT AND WINDER

Lake Poinsett west of Cocoa has numerous bass among the reeds that grow in four feet of water and less. The bottom is generally sand or a thin layer of muck over sand. The lake's bass fishing is variable, as is the angling in the canals along the east side of Poinsett. Several areas on the lake produce schooling bass in the spring and summer months. The river mouth as it enters the lake is one of the best spots to find that action. Waters there vary from three to five feet deep.

South of Poinsett lie some productive river stretches that are sometimes almost dry during extreme drought conditions. The dropoff on the outer bend of the river at the mouth of the sloughs off this section of river yields largemouth in the summer. Concentrate on the water ranging from 3 to 10 feet deep off the vegetation. Also check out the river bends, especially around profuse aquatic vegetation.

Lake Winder is small, with expanses of hydrilla that yield lots of small largemouth from the cover in four feet of water. Fish the shallow vegetation on the west side of the lake for schooling bass in the late spring and early summer. Schoolers often move onto the grassy points in the afternoons. The river mouth can also provide bass action in the summer and fall months.

Fishing pressure is nil on the river either side of Winder, and small two-pound bass seem to school there relatively unbothered. This area of the river offers sloughs and false channels with bulrush and reed points in 2 to 4 feet of water. It's good spring and fall bass fishing at the mouths of these sloughs when the water level is normal to high. Trophy bass are present during spring spawning.

The upper St. Johns River bass angling is a secret to many. With high water, most of it is navigable. During a drought, though, you can forget about fishing much of the river area between the lakes. The river normally provides good angling during the wetter months when the water is up. Those stretches of knee-deep river and adjacent sloughs can produce bass even though they are extremely shallow.

Lake Washington & Upstream

Lake Washington has a low level weir at the exit of the river which helps keep water in the lake. The crest of the weir is at 13.5 feet above sea level, and when water levels are lower than this, downstream flow stops. The section of river between Lakes Winder and Washington is the steepest gradient section of the entire St. Johns River. Because of the weir and high gradient, that portion of the river becomes completely dewatered during extended low water conditions. Lake Washington produces bass even though it is shallow most of the year.

Lakes Hellen Blazes and Sawgrass near the headwaters both provide good bass angling in the fall and spring months when the water is up. Droughts occur every three or four years on the upper river, and super-shallow lakes Hellen Blazes and Sawgrass can get extremely low during dry periods.

Live Bait Tactics

Cool weather bass often show a preference for large river shiners served in the deep outer bends, while hot weather largemouth frequently 'school up' on the numerous sandbars along the 25 to 70 foot wide river. Knowing where to look is the key to finding bass of any size.

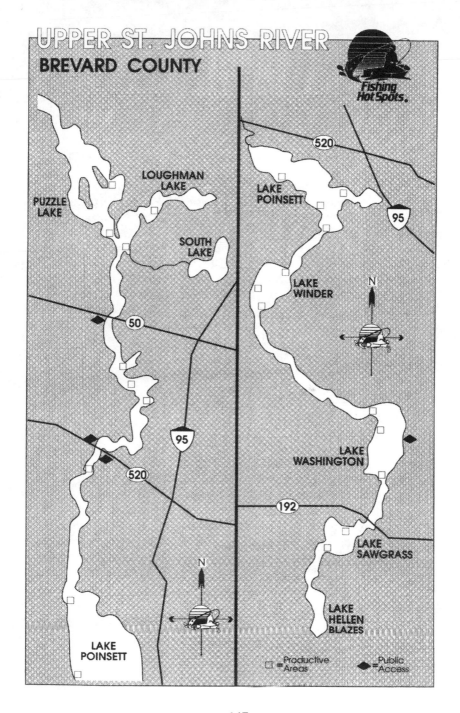

In 30 years of fishing the headwaters of the St. Johns, Stonewater has learned how to identify areas with the highest fishing potential. He has learned the "ways of a river" just by spending thousands of days on it. His abilities to "read" the waters are not unlike those of other "river rats" around the state.

"You have to realize what the current does, where it hits, where the drop offs are formed, and how the structure may be piled up on the bottom," he told me as we slowed at a bend in the river and glided into the mouth of a small incoming slough. "You need to be able to determine how the bottom slopes and where the current turns. That's where the submerged trees will pile up."

On that particular trip, my wife, Lilliam, came along, eager to catch a big fish. The slough, near highway 50, looked to me like it could produce a lunker bass. Bob evidently knew that it would.

The slough was deep with an active flowage from the river channel. The quick drop off down to 12 feet of water made the opposite bank ideal for trophy bass that move up to trap forage against it. A weed patch cover extending 3 feet out from the shoreline and eel grass nearby on the inner bend of the river set the stage. The affable guide and his clients have caught nine bass over 13 pounds from similar river stretches.

"Anglers won't generally go into places that are only 10 feet wide, but the lunker bass will," explained Stonewater. "It's not the size of the creek, but the depth of water, amount of current and the cover present that's important."

Several big bass were in this spot as it turned out. They were laying out of the current and ready to feed. Lilliam's first cast was sucked in by a six pounder and the battle was on. The fish was quickly put into the live well to keep the shiners company and to hold for pictures later. Stonewater passed his rod to my wife for two more largemouth between five and seven pounds.

My shiner always seemed to avoid the big fish that morning. We had some exciting action at the bank as the big bass would try to pin the baitfish against the cover. Finally, the big one hit - Lilliam's shiner. The eight and one-half pounder was her largest ever and made her a confirmed bass angler for life, I believe.

Our morning was similar to others that I've had on the upper river with Stonewater. At least a half dozen bass from around three to seven pounds were also caught and released. I've fished several times with him on the 50-mile stretch of headwaters, and always caught nice bass.

The river is not the most beautiful in terms of shoreline cover, but the author usually finds it productive.

Lure Tactics & Giants

Tossing artificials also can work well in the river over prime habitat. Big crankbaits, vibrating plugs and plastic worms with a slow wiggle produce bass-attracting sound waves on these waters. Small, tight-wiggling lures catch small river bass, while big bass go for the larger lures. Angling is very productive with the swimming worm rig, an open-hook six inch worm with a kink at the bend.

Most of the bass, regardless of size, lie along brushy or highly vegetated banks just after a rain shower. As the water flow increases in the river or tributaries, bass move into the natural feeding holes with current. Forage is washed into the river, and it's usually hugging the shoreline tightly as it washes downstream.

Your cast will have to present the lure close to any river monster. They seldom move far to feed, preferring an area with some current that will wash forage to them. You may have to cast prime river structure 30 times and return to the same spot four or five times during the day to catch a lunker. A big fish will eat a mouthful and then might not feed the rest of that day.

You just can't predict when a river lunker will hit an artificial lure. Smaller St. Johns largemouth may actively feed several times a day, but the trophies feed primarily on big items that are worth the chase. Big river largemouth do feed year around, however, and there's usually always some bass feeding in the better river areas.

In general, high water allows fish to disperse into all the river and into the floodplain marsh. Low water levels concentrated bass in the deeper river sections and mainstream lakes. When it's hot, largemouth bass activity shifts from the shallow vegetated areas. Higher pH levels in the thin waters cause an adjustment to slightly deeper waters, to more shaded waters and to those in current. Schools of largemouth may move offshore in the deeper waters of a lake. In fact, schooling bass push panicky shad to the surface frequently in July and August.

Schoolers can be found around the deeper channels where the St. Johns enters and leaves the lakes, where other tributaries and sloughs enter the river and, sometimes, at wide spots in the river. School bass are most likely to be breaking water in the mornings, evenings, just before afternoon thunderstorms and sometimes during overcast weather. Try a vibrating plug or topwater lure when the activity is on top.

The St. Johns near the headwaters offers probably the most overlooked, quality fishery in the state. This section of the river system just doesn't get a lot of pressure fortunately, but it still pays to be conservation minded. I release all of what I catch there. Trophy bass fishing success here is enjoyed by many due to local anglers and guides encouraging voluntary catch and release.

In the spring, giant spawning bass are pursued by more anglers, and when the fishing grounds are so narrow, heavy angling activities and boat traffic can hamper productive trips. During the rest of the year, only cattle trespass along the water road loaded with bass.

RIVER DETAILS

The headwaters of the upper St. Johns River begin in the marsh surrounding Blue Cypress Lake. From there, it meanders slowly through lowland swamps, wetlands and lakes Hellen Blazes, Sawgrass, Little Lake Sawgrass, Ruth, Clark, Loughman, Washington, Winder and Poinsett. The latter three large lakes average five to six foot depth and the others about three. Washington, Winder and Poinsett all have maximum depths of around nine feet.

Lake	Acreage
Hellen Blazes	381
Little Lake Sawgrass	74
Sawgrass	407
Washington	4,362
Winder	1,496
Poinsett	4,334
Ruth, Clark and Loughman	950

You'll find shoreline and slough-bound vegetation such as hydrilla, water hyacinth, coontail, eelgrass, water shield, spatterdock and bulrushes throughout this section of the St. Johns River system. The two lakes most affected by hydrilla are Lake Hellen Blazes and Sawgrass Lake, but most of the others have plenty. Bass in the lakes hang out around the emergent rushes, when water depth is sufficient, and in the submerged hydrilla when waters are low. Bass in the river are found around willow, coontail and/or pennywort.

There are some public points of access along the river. On the east side of the river in Brevard County a very remote ramp at the Hatbill Park. It lies several miles south of Highway 46 and is used primarily by 4-wheel drive vehicles with lightweight boats or airboats. A much better launch area lies on the southwest side of the Highway 50 bridge on the river. Another small one can be found off Highway 520 on the northwest side of the bridge.

The best free public ramp area on this part of the river lies off Highway 520 on the east side. The James Bourbeau Memorial Park has a nice double concrete ramp and fairly complete facilities (not found elsewhere along this stretch of the river). On the east side of Lake Washington in Melbourne off Lake Washington Road is an unimproved ramp suitable mainly for those in a 4-wheel drive vehicle. Guide service is available through Bob Stonewater's Trophy Bass Guide Service, 179 Glenwood Rd., DeLand, FL 32720; phone (904) 736-7120.

16

SOUTH SWAMPLANDS, FOREVER GLADES

TO BASS IN THE Everglades, spillway runoffs provide an endless food supply. Moving water is a natural attraction, but not all anglers realize the advantages of the flow. Food washing into a canal, creek or river area is the draw, and the advantages of locating a concentrated group of feeding fish are obvious.

The often fat and healthy specimens are uniformly positioned for grabbing the forage morsels, and then they are generally shallower than at other times. While moving water in the 'glades is generally rich in nutrients, it is also usually cooler and more oxygenated. With the abundant food supply, the fish won't have to spend much energy chasing after smaller members of the food chain. The result is larger fish in such locations. When they have first shot at the supply, why wouldn't they grow faster and bigger.

The opportunities for catching freshwater bass species are many in southern Florida.

I had an interesting experience on my first trip to the Ten Thousand Islands area of the 2,200 square mile Everglades National Park. The park is the second largest national park in the contiguous 48 states. The Everglades are often called Florida's "last fishing frontier." Nestled into the Gulf of Mexico lie more than 1 1/2 million acres of unspoiled park land and waters teeming with fish. The Ten Thousands Islands area, located between Miami and Naples, has some of the best snook, tarpon, trout and redfish angling in the state. Overlooked in the hundreds of miles of irrigation canals along and off the Tamiami Trail and in the glades-draining tributaries, though, are largemouth bass.

Takeoff point for some of the bass angling is the marina and boat launching facilities at the Port of the Islands Harbor. The harbor, lying just off the Faka Union River, is a manatee sanctuary that also contains plenty of tarpon, and at times, largemouth beneath the dam. Just upstream of the harbor is a small reservoir full of largemouth.

The Faka Union River water is brackish and affected by the tides below the reservoir dam. The small dam spreads across one of the many tributaries which dumps fresh Conservation Area waters into the finger-like bays of the Gulf of Mexico. The swirling water beneath the concrete structure frequently holds some largemouth.

The water is brackish, but the salinity that day was low enough for the freshwater bass. I cautiously moved up toward the dam, tossing a Mepp's spinner. My third cast resulted in a smashing strike and a high flying snook.

I released the 17 incher and cast again. I worked the bait near the rocky bottom knowing not only of the possible snags but also of the bass that await. A two pound largemouth struck at it, and after three leaps skyward and a good tussle in the fast current, it was brought aboard to try out the live well. In the following ten minutes, I caught another two largemouth, a twin to my first snook, and missed a couple of good strikes.

The action below the dam slowed, so I began thinking of how to find some additional bass. The boat was anchored about 30 feet from the dam structure and the bottom shallowed up, reaching near the surface in a couple of areas just below the dam. I had thoroughly worked most of the water in the spillway with a variety of lures, and it was time to try something new.

I noticed some productive-looking cover on the shore just above the dam. The surface of the water was about eye-level and I had no idea how deep it was on the other side, but it was worth losing a lure to find out! I tossed a Little George as far as I could along the shoreline above the dam. I half-way expected a hang-up before my retrieve had reached the dam, and surely anticipated hooking the top of the dam if the lure got that far.

I had retrieved the heavy tail-spinner lure about 20 feet when the rod was jolted by the sudden attack of a hungry largemouth. The three pounder jumped twice before I worked her to the dam. The third time I saw her was when I 'horsed' her over the dam. She fell six feet down into the white water as I frantically reeled to take up the event's resulting slack.

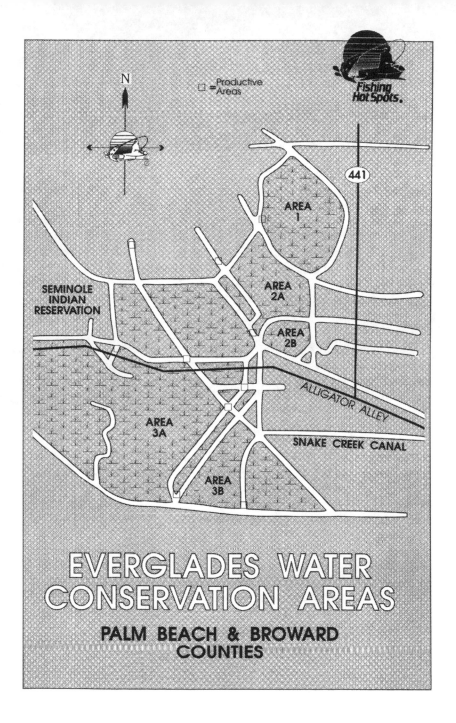

□ = Productive Areas

N

441

Fishing Hot Spots.

AREA 1

AREA 2A

AREA 2B

SEMINOLE INDIAN RESERVATION

ALLIGATOR ALLEY

AREA 3A

SNAKE CREEK CANAL

AREA 3B

EVERGLADES WATER CONSERVATION AREAS

PALM BEACH & BROWARD COUNTIES

I gained control again and led her out of the rocks and to the boat. My net helped her into the live well. That's something I thought; I'll have to try that again. My next three casts were unproductive, but I did get my lure to scoot across the dam without a hang-up. My following cast gained another strike, however, and a two pound bass was soon tumbling over the dam. The lure was dislodged in the fall, though.

Not to be discouraged, I kept tossing and in the following hour, caught three more dare-devil bass. My catch from the challenging obstacle was sizable, yet I had lost only one lure in the rocks below the dam and one to a snag above the structure. The ease with which the lure and hooked bass could be brought over the dam was surprising. Even the great angling opportunity that existed to a caster willing to try was, to me, surprising. When 99 percent of the anglers thoroughly fish out the spillway, they leave. From that day on, I've continued to cast above the structure to check it out.

Tackle Considerations

A successful angler fishing the South Florida runoffs will be a line watcher. Due to water turbulence beneath dams and canal water control structures, a careful eye on the monofilament is vital. My line weights vary from 14 pound test to 17 for normal situations. Bass in these conditions have little time to spot the line or to detect a counterfeit bait.

Lure selection is, however, very important. Crankbaits are excellent choices in these moving water areas, and shad-colored deep-running billed lures are favorites. I'll always lean toward a shad or crayfish imitation in these forage-intensive places. Chrome sides and brown crayfish patterns that run three to eight feet down take their share of largemouth cranked from swirling water.

White 1/4 to 3/8 lead head jigs with white plastic curl tails are also effective. Jiggin' spoons can be bounced along the bottom for a good share of the bass market. Again, the lure may just stop, so be prepared to strike back. Tail-spinner baits and weedless Texas-rigged worms also pull their share in these fishy areas. Curly-tail wigglers in a seven-inch length are productive. Lures should get down quick in the moving water and resemble forage.

Everglades Sawgrass Bass

The 4.3 million acre Everglades, often called "River of Grass," is the largest freshwater system in South Florida. In 1948, it was divided up into the three easily-accessible reservoir Wildlife

Big topwater plugs fished along canal bank vegetation can result in a big bass.

Management Areas that exist today. Conservation Area Number 3 (914 square miles) is in Dade and Broward counties north of Highway 41 and west of Highway 27. Conservation Area Number 2 (210 square miles) is east of Highway 27 in Broward County, and Conservation Area Number 1 (221 square miles) is also called the Loxahatchee National Wildlife Refuge.

Three major entries to the Everglades, one at each conservation area, are the Everglades Holiday Park on Highway 27, Sawgrass Recreation Area on Highway 84, and the Loxahatchee Recreation Area off Highway 441. Thus, the conservation areas attract most of the fishing pressure in the Everglades. For a map, write the South Florida Water Management District.

The 2,400 square mile Big Cypress National Preserve, Miccosukee Indian Reservation, Seminole Indian Reservation, Fakahatchee Strand State Preserve, Rotenberger Wildlife Management Area and other smaller areas are also in the 'glades.

About 1,400 miles of canals criss-crossing most of the vast, governmental-controlled areas offer prime bass fishing opportunities. You can fish those alongside a road from the bank, but you'll need a boat to access the others running into the marsh. On the water, you options are canal fishing or, if you have an airboat, backcountry exploring. There are very few directional signs and numerous unmarked ditches in the swamplands of South Florida.

Canals bearing designations such as C-17 or L-68 are among hundreds that have been dug throughout South Florida since the early part of the century. Drainage Districts, the South Florida Water Management District, cities and even private developments have designed levees and dikes to set up the narrow bass waterways. The water in may can be fairly clear, particularly during low water times.

The majority of the bass-rich canals in this part of the state were dug in the 50s and 60s, but the major canals, the Tamiami, North New River and West Palm Beach, were dug between 1905 and 1920. Most were dug to drain the Everglades, and today most all of them have water control structures to regulate levels (to keep water from draining). Although the area receives an average of 55 inches of annual rainfall, conservation of water today is the priority.

County and state agencies have laid several decent launching pads on some of the canals, so access is possible on many. Smaller craft and those trailered behind 4-wheel drive vehicles are best suited for accessing most. Some are in bad shape and some provide little more than a ditch path to the water. There is no accurate record of where the launch areas are, so it may take some prowling to locate the one suited for your next trip into "Sawgrass Country."

The 84-mile long Alligator Alley (Highway 84) canal, like many in the Everglades Conservation Areas of Dade, Broward and Palm Beach Counties, is box-cut with steep banks and a level bottom. It is about 40 feet wide and well over 30 feet deep. Bass fishing in this canal during times of drought is especially productive. Largemouth pull out of shallow marshes and ditches, and concentrate in the deep-water canal areas. There is sometimes very little littoral zone, as fishery biologists call the vegetated food shelf. In fact, the box-cut was designed to inhibit growth of aquatic plants.

Other Glades Spots

The L-28 intercept canal off the Alligator Alley is like some canals in that it has areas deeper than others. Those variances are due to dragline operators making a few extra scoops, or turning around or changing course. They can be found with the aid of a sonar unit. Such remote areas are productive in hot or cold weather. Check out any running water during other times.

Canal intersections, water control structures and holes in dikes are the hot spots. Rainy days are, obviously, often productive times on these canals. An average of 50 inches of rain falls on the Everglades each year. Also the cuts and alligator den entrances often hold good-sized bass.

Keep the bass head up and out of the canal's entanglements, and you'll land it.

The feeder or intercept canals that run through the Conservation Areas are usually most productive, because they get the least angler traffic. While most canals are 12 feet deep, many are 15 to 20 feet deep. Many have holes in them that may drop from 25 to 30 feet. Most have productive ledges along their banks. The vegetated berms, culverts, bridges, flood gates and sandbars throughout the system are other good spots that congregate largemouth.

The Tamiami Trail (Highway 41) Canal yields good bass at times, despite heavy fishing pressure. One of the better canals is the L-67 Canal between the Tamiami Trial and the Everglades Holiday Park. It yields big bass at times. Another that does is the Sunshine State Turnpike canal, which runs the South Florida portion of the toll road. Lots of bass over 10 pounds have been taken from this often overlooked waterway. The eastern part of the Tamiami Trail Canal is the most popular area in this waterway. The 40-Mile Bend area is another active area that seems to produce lots of bass.

Other canals to check out are the Miami Canal and the New River Canal (Highway 27) that run from Lake Okeechobee through the Conservation Areas. The Ocean Canal (Highway 441) is another good bass waterway all the way from the "Big O" to Royal Palm Beach. The drainage canals along the farm roads around the big lake are good fishing areas too.

The Carnestown (Intersection of Highways 29 and 41) Canal area, the Royal Palm Hammock canal area and the Turner's River Canal near Marco are other spots that often offer bass in brackish waters. Mercury contamination in some glades areas makes it unwise to eat any fish. That's why catch-and-release fishing is gaining popularity in the sawgrass region. In fact, this area has one of the highest voluntary live release rates to total bass catch of any waters in the state.

The Holiday Park attraction and launch site is a good starting point for the newcomer to glades bassin'. It's located in Conservation Area 3(A) just south of Highway 84 at the intersection of Griffin Road and Highway 27, and boating the four or five canals away from it is safe. You can't get lost very easily. The alternative is to arrange for an experienced guide when boating off the beaten path.

Sawgrass Park, located off Highway 27 about two miles north of Interstate Highway 75 in the Conservation Area Number 2 west of Fort Lauderdale, has numerous sawgrass-lined canals that contain good bass fishing. It's smaller than the Holiday Park operation, but there's a marina and launch ramp at this "island" in the glades. Narrow roadways lead to other smaller "islands" on all sides of the Park activity center. Fee camping on the smaller islands is available.

The Big Cypress National Preserve has several natural potholes which are productive in times of relatively low water. Small ponds between the cypress and oak hammocks hold lots of bass, but it may take an airboat to access them. Some of those who do get into them report fantastic bass fishing!

Loxahatchee Wilderness

Some call the 25-mile long Loxahatchee west of Jupiter off Highway 706 the last wild and scenic river in South Florida. For bass anglers with a canoe or small boat, this river provides a unique, wonderful experience. The river varies from five to 30 feet in the areas of good float fishing.

The Indian name means "river of turtles." The numerous cypress knees along the river banks give turtles ample opportunity for sunning themselves. Cypress trees hundreds of years old form a canopy over many stretches of the twisting waterway from River Bend Park to Jonathan Dickinson State Park almost eight miles. Brazilian pepper and Australian Pine trees, commonly found in southeast Florida, are numerous along the waterway too. Ferns, vines and bushes skirt the river banks, so casting accuracy is vital in the tight spaces along the primitive Loxahatchee.

160

For the first couple of miles, the bow-positioned angler will have suitable casting targets. The river is overgrown and narrow, and the stern man needs to be most concerned with navigation through the tiny places. Bass will be concentrated in the deeper pools, and it is best to just fish from pool to pool, paying little attention to the shallows in between.

The river opens to around 60 feet near the Sunshine State Parkway Turnpike bridge, so both can easily fish downstream after that. It's about three to four miles from the bridge to the famous Trapper Nelson's hunting camp and zoo, and the State Park. The river in that area is wide and the current fairly slow. Fishing further for largemouth is spotty.

The 70-square mile Loxahatchee Basin is half-fresh and half-salt water, but the best bass fishing is in the narrow 10-mile stretch out of the Loxahatchee Slough near the River Bend Park. Spots to toss a small spinner or plastic worm are the mouths of the two tributaries, Cypress Creek and Kitching Creek. Use spinning gear and small lures for the relatively small bass you'll find along this waterway. The scenery and wilderness experience is what you'll remember about this trip, not the bass fishing.

Martin Cooling Pond

Resident bass anglers have a unique opportunity to fish the normally off-limits Martin Power Plant Cooling Pond and benefit the United Way while doing so. Florida Power and Light Company has granted the charity permission to conduct a "Fishing For Fun" event on four two-day periods throughout each year.

The bass fishing in the 5,000-acre warm water reservoir near Indiantown is among the best in the state. Only Florida residents may participate in the United Way benefits scheduled for weekends in September, November, January and April of each year.

The combination of warm water, excellent habitat and restricted access make for great bass fishing, and many more applications than the established quota selected for each of the eight days are received by officials. Special permits are drawn for the weekends, and a donation of $175 per boat is required. If selected, up to 3 people (Florida residents only) can fish from a boat. Only about 60 boats are allowed each of the eight days.

For more information or applications to fish the Indiantown impoundment during one of those weekends, contact the United Way of Martin County, P.O. Box 362, Stuart, FL 34995 or by calling (407) 283-4800.

Osborne's Sunshine Option

Water temperatures in the low 60's mean one thing to a growing fraternity of South Florida anglers - hybrid striped bass. The cold weather slows down forage fish which results in a great opportunity for the roving schools of sunshine bass, as the cross between the striper and white bass is called. South Florida offers some great areas for catching sunshine bass.

Lake Osborne in Palm Beach County is a good bet for action, according to Tom Vaughn, Chief of Fisheries for the Game and Fresh Water Fish Commission. The water temperature and flow there tends to congregate sunshines, particularly at the Sixth Avenue, Lantana and Keller Canal bridges.

There are other hot fishing areas as well. The Commission stocks approximately 1.7 million sunshines annually into 174,000 acres of lakes and 430 miles of rivers throughout the state. While not all South Florida waters have the aggressive open water feeders, there is usually sunshine bass available within a short drive.

Sunshine bass will hit any artificial lure that resembles a shad. Tail spinners, in-line spinners, spoons, crank baits, vibrating plugs, and plastic grubs can be extremely seductive to the hard-hitting and fighting sunshines. Naturally, live shad and minnows are productive for bait fishermen. They continue to hit well until the spring waters begin to warm.

Sunshines are light-sensitive and generally move shallower on cloudy days to feed. Bright sun rays which penetrate deep into the water will usually drive the fish down. Early morning, late evening, windy and rainy days can all be highly productive, as the larger hybrids can be round nearer the surface.

17

MIAMI CONNECTIONS

THE NEW FISH down in the Miami area is a battler. It's an urban fish that provides new recreational opportunities in southeast Florida for families. The peacock bass readily takes live bait and is particularly suited for children, according to Paul Shafland, a biologist with the Game and Fresh Water Fish Commission, and Director of their Non-Native Fish Research Laboratory.

"A man called me the other day and said that they had just held a kid's tournament on a small pond off one of the Miami canals," relates Shafland, "and almost 60 pounds of peacock bass were caught. Those fish were taken by children fishing from the bank mostly with live bait."

Over 1,000 miles of freshwater canals in South Florida now boast a thriving population of peacock bass.

For those more avid anglers, the peacock bass readily strikes most artificial lures, and that can result in multiple hook-ups. The schooling fish often follow a hooked fish to the boat. Another lure tossed to the area may result in a second fish hooked. Some anglers have caught two of the brightly-colored peacock bass on the same plug, one on each treble hook. Peacock bass have an insatiable appetite and will forage on whatever is available.

The bag limit is two butterfly peacock bass, only one of which can be greater than 17 inches. The speckled peacock species is currently a catch-and-release fish only. The distribution of each is limited to the fresh waters in the southeast part of Florida, primarily in Dade and southern Broward counties. The entire canal system is interconnected, however, and the primary range of the peacock is about 70 miles long by 35 miles wide, encompassing well over 1,000 miles of canals.

The fish was initially stocked in 10 canals from the Homestead area north to around Pompano Beach in October of 1984. Over 1,100 butterfly peacocks approximately two inches in length were released, and today the average size of peacock bass caught is one to two pounds. A few trophies weighing up to seven pounds have been taken by the urban anglers. Catch rates in the canal system for black bass, almost one every two hours, is about double other state waters. Peacock bass catch rates are about twice that, or about .80 fish per hour.

South Florida water control structures every 10 miles or so limit boat travel to the portion of canal one launches on. Some areas offer excellent concrete ramps for large boats, while others are more suitable for a car topper or lightweight johnboat. Many canals are tiny with limited access, while other larger systems accommodate up to 300 man-hours per acre of angling pressure, according to Shafland.

Many of the canals intersect each other, and some are connected to small lakes. Some of the canals around Miami are not located in the best of neighborhoods, so get local advice regarding launching sites. Many of the canals are surprisingly clean and very clear with visibility to 15 feet. Most are uniformly 15 feet deep and have a sharp dropoff at the shoreline.

Several South Florida canals provide good fishing. The Mowry Canal in south Dade County and Snake Creek at the Dade-Broward County line are a couple of waterways with excellent peacock bass fishing. Others without names are even better, and some small lakes connecting to the canal system offer good peacock bass fishing as well. The lakes near the Miami International Airport are good examples.

Peacock Identification and Lifestyle

The common English name, peacock bass, is derived by Americans from the common Spanish name, "pavon" (which means peacock). While the peacock resembles the largemouth in action, the two are genetically far apart. The largemouth is a sunfish and the peacock is a cichla.

The butterfly peacock has three vertical bars in its early years and then, the bars tend to fade. The fish's base color can vary from green to gold. The speckled peacock is a dark olive green color with four to six prominent horizontal lines. Older fish have less dramatic coloration, turn gold and develop three very prominent

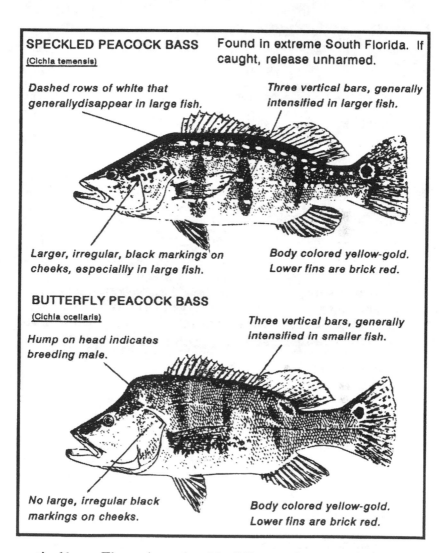

SPECKLED PEACOCK BASS
(Cichla temensis)

Found in extreme South Florida. If caught, release unharmed.

Dashed rows of white that generally disappear in large fish.

Three vertical bars, generally intensified in larger fish.

Larger, irregular, black markings on cheeks, especiallly in large fish.

Body colored yellow-gold. Lower fins are brick red.

BUTTERFLY PEACOCK BASS
(Cichla ocellaris)

Hump on head indicates breeding male.

Three vertical bars, generally intensified in smaller fish.

No large, irregular black markings on cheeks.

Body colored yellow-gold. Lower fins are brick red.

vertical bars. The main noticeable difference between the speckled and the butterfly is the black blotches on the cheek plates of the speckled peacock.

The peacock is very temperature-dependent, and as a result is limited in range. It dies at 60 degrees. The water temperature in the canals seldom fall below 70 degrees, and the lowest recorded in the past nine years was 66 degrees. The box-cut canals expose

The average size of peacock bass caught in the Dade County canals is around 1 pound.

relatively small amounts of the water to colder air temperatures and are responsible for the ideal over-wintering environment.

Small live shiners attract peacock bass readily under most conditions. Anglers using live bait will usually outfish those tossing artificials. Fly fishermen and those purists lure tosser will find topwater minnow plugs, surface baits with spinners and jigs all work well. Once hooked, the peacocks are extremely active and will jump several times.

A few speckled peacocks are swimming around the Dade and Broward County waters, but their numbers are few. The butterfly is considered established and a permanent species in the canals. The speckled peacock has been introduced in lesser numbers and takes three years to become sexually mature, which limits its abundance. The butterfly, on the other hand, are sexually mature in just one year when they are about 12 inches in length. Many have spawned naturally several times in the canals.

Canal Forage Base

The speckled peacock were introduced because they grow large and may provide a trophy fishery. The butterfly peacock may well be South Florida's bread-and-butter-type fish that will complement the existing largemouth bass fishery in the canals. Creel checks thus far have found the butterfly to offer similar size distributions as the largemouth. The butterfly should be more successful numerically than the largemouth, though, according to Shafland.

The dense population of spotted tilapia and other exotic food fish in the canals is important to the growth of the fishery. The

166

Peacock bass in South Florida are feisty, as the author's wife, Lilliam, finds out.

canal-based forage fish average about 13 pounds for every one pound of predator fish. Normally, four or five pounds of forage to one pound of predator is considered ideal by biologists.

"The peacocks are not expected to displace the current bass population," explains biologist Paul Shafland, "but rather supplement largemouth by helping them reduce the number of overly abundant forage."

Stocking the peacocks in the canal system of South Florida was partially based on it being the right habitat and upon the fish's ability to help harvest over-abundant baitfish. By introducing peacock bass, spotted tilapia, which comprises about 25 percent of the forage base by number and weight, is more effectively utilized. In the canal system, a four-pound peacock may represent up to 40 pounds of forage fish that it has eaten, according to Shafland.

Thus, a very abundant resource is converted into a highly utilizable game fish, the peacock bass. For more information on the Florida peacock fishery, contact: Paul Shafland, Director, Non-Native Fish Research Laboratory, Florida Game and Fresh Water Fish Commission, 801 N.W. 40th St., Boca Raton, FL 33431 or phone (407) 391-6409.

City Opportunities

The canals of urban Miami are a latticework designed for drainage, but they are also utilized by many as a dependable bass fishery. The man-made waterways offer endless fishing opportunities to the urban explorer. The Airport Lakes system,

There are plenty of opportunities to catch bass from the canals in southeast Florida.

centered around Miami International Airport is a shining example of the fishing in Dade County.

The Airport Lakes, south of Miami's East-West Expressway (Highway 836), contain numerous different lakes covering several hundred acres. They are linked to canals and other small lakes throughout several older suburb neighborhoods. Largemouth and peacocks are in all of them. Many of the lakes are 40 and 50 feet deep, so the big bass are often in those depths.

The shoreline cover, particularly on the south shore of the main lake, also harbors largemouth most of the year. Ledges and emergent vegetation offer bass the habitat they need in lakes surrounded by development. Fish the clearer, shallow waters early and late in the day and the deep holes and drops after the sun is high. Water clarity in the Airport Lakes is often like glass, so the careful approach to a fishing hole is wise.

Lake anglers may want to schedule their bass trips on weekdays, when the weekend crowds of pleasure boaters and water skiers don't have to be dealt with. The primary navigation problem for big bass boats and tall anglers are the low bridges on some of the backyard canals. The bridges, however, are excellent bass hangouts. Fish them and any culverts you come across in the exploration.

The developments of South Florida often have bank access to canals and small ponds where largemouth lurk.

The ramp into the Airport Lakes system is on the main lake, just behind an airport parking lot. Other launch ramps exist in the area, but many are in sorry state. Four-wheel drive vehicles are wise in most of the off-the-main-track access areas. Safety of the vehicles left at many ramp sites while fishing has been a problem.

The Aerojet Canal (C-111) is one that usually provide good bass action. The waterway, that begins east of Everglades National Park and flows southeast into Manatee Bay, was dug in the mid-sixties. It is deeper and wider than most in rural South Dade County. Anticipated barge traffic to a rocket engine test site provided the incentive for such a large-scale canal. That never happened, but numerous smaller canals were tied into the C-111 afterwards.

An earthen dam east of the Highway 1 bridge prevents saltwater intrusion. A good boat ramp on the freshwater side of the dam is not crowded most weekdays. A road runs along one side of a portion of the canal, so bank fishing may be possible.

Much of the action is at the intersections of tributary canal culverts. Bass are there for the flowing water and food source provided by such. The waters here are also very clear, so stealth may give you an advantage. There are some sloughs along the canal that produce small to mid-size bass. Check them out.

The canal waters around Miami are kept relatively clear of vegetation by the Water Management District. As a result, bass are often in deep water beside the sharp dropoff. Waters may be contained or flowing in either direction, depending on conservation requirements of the District.

DEVELOPMENT BASS

As the weather begins to cool some, largemouth in the Gold Coast's small waters become more active. Since Broward and other nearby counties are blessed (or cursed) with rapid development, those waters created or enhanced by real estate developers are often bass hotspots in the spring and fall.

Golf, country club and luxury home developments are places to find hungry largemouth, and there are literally hundreds spread around the area. Some of the waters are off-limits to the public, but the majority are open to all. Permission to fish can usually be obtained from a homeowner, property manager or caretaker.

Golf courses are sometimes closed down for a day each week, offering a chance for anglers to obtain approval to fish. Access from the bank or small boat is possible even in golf course ponds (water hazards), provided you don't interfere with those members playing golf.

In most South Florida development waters, fishing pressure is minimal and there is very little publicity about what is caught. Attention to fish management techniques is often exemplified at golf country clubs, residential and resort complexes. The quality of bass fishing in the small lakes is directly related to the efforts of the architects and manager. Many such lakes were designed and developed utilizing proven fishery methods to provide the unlimited sport fishing opportunities.

Many of this region's esthetic development waterways have sand bottoms and adequate vegetation for cover of prey and predator alike. Apartment, condominium and home developments often offer the amenities of nicely landscaped waterways, many of which are loaded with bass that have little exposure to man.

APPENDICES

APPENDIX A

South Florida Water Bodies & Acreage

Brevard County

Clark Lake	182
Fox Lake	185
Lake Hellen Blazes	381
Lake Poinsett	4,334
Lake Sawgrass	407
Lake Washington	4,362
Lake Winder	1,496
Little Lake Sawgrass	74
Loughman Lake	557
Ruth Lake	210
Salt Lake	366
South Lake	1,101

Broward County

Broward County Lake	1,270
Coconut Creek	60
Lauderdale Lakes	90
Lauderhill Lakes	134
Margate Lakes	255
Miramar Lakes	72
Oakland Park Lakes	109
Tamarac Lakes	549
West Ft. Lauderdale WMD	120

Charlotte County

Prairie Creek	40
Shell Creek	48
Shell/Prairie Creek Res.	140

Collier County

Waterways	5,298
Lake Trafford	1,494

Dade County

Waterways	1,250

Hardee County

Peace River	150

Hendry County

Waterways	325

Highlands County

Lake Apthorpe	219
Arbuckle Creek	120
Clay Lake	467
Dinner Lake	379
Lake Glenada	150
Grassey Lake	517
Lake Huntley	500
Lake Istokpoga	27,692
Lake Jackson	3,400
Lake June in Winter	3,504
Lake Lelia	165
Letta Lake	478
Little Red Water Lake	329
Lake Lotela	802
Lake Placid Canals	250
Lake Placid	3,320
Red Beach Lake	355
Lake Sebring	468

Indian River County

Blue Cypress Lake	6,555
Fellsmere	531
Indian River Farms	392
Farm 13	6,000

Lee County

Caloosahatchee River	20,000
East Lee County	488
Lee County Hyacinth	1,300

Manatee County

Bill Evers Reservoir	269
Braden River	220
County Waterways	3,111
Manatee River	30
Lake Manatee	1,550

Okeechobee County

Lake Okeechobee	448,000

Osceola County

Lake Ajay 145
Alligator Lake 3 .... ,406
Bay Lake 110
Boggy Creek 18
Brick Lake 616
Lake Center 410
Coon Lake 148
Cypress Lake 4,097
East Lake
    Tohopekaliga 12,546
Fish Lake 221
Lake Gentry 1,791
Lake Hatchineha 6,665
Lake Jackson 1,020
Kissimmee River 4,240
Lake Kissimmee 34,948
Lake Lizzie 792
Lake Marian 5,739
Runnymede Lake 300
Lake Trout 273
Lake Tohopekaliga 18,810

Palm Beach County

West Palm Beach
    City Waterways 242
Lake Ida 159
Indian Trail 608
Lake Clarke Shores 150
Lake Worth 1,703
Loxahatchee WCD 237
Loxahatchee River 100
Lake Mangonia 540
North County WCD 843
Lake Osborne 56
Seminole WCD 4,000

Polk County

Lake Agnes 386
Lake Alfred 736
Lake Annie 539
Lake Arbuckle 3,828
Lake Ariana 1,026
Banana Lake 342
Lake Bonnet 78
Lake Bonny 354
Buckeye Lake 71
Lake Buffum 1,543
Cannon Lake 336
Lake Clinch 1,207
Lake Conine 236
Crooked Lake 5,538
Deer Lake 125
Eagle Lake 651
Lake Elbert 173

Lake Eloise 1,160
Eva Lake 176
Lake Garfield 655
Lake Haines 716
Lake Hamilton 2,126
Lake Hancock 4,519
Lake Hartridge 434
Lake Hollingsworth 356
Lake Howard 628
Lake Hunter 100
Lake Idylwild 102
Lake Jessie 190
Lake Juliana 926
Lake Lena 207
Little Lake Hamilton 367
Lake Livingston 1,203
Lake Lowery 815
Lake Lulu 301
Lake Mariana 500
Lake Marion 2,990
Lake Mattie 1,078
Lake May 44
Middle Lake Hamilton 106
Lake Mirror 123
Lake Moody 391
Mud Lake 133
Lake Parker 2,272
Lake Patrick 393
Lake Pierce 3,729
Lake Reedy 3,486
Lake Rochelle 578
Lake Rosalie 4,597
Lake Roy ..?.. 78
Saddle Creek 30
Lake Shipp 263
Smart Lake 275
Lake Spring 25
Lake Summit 67
Swoope Lake 112
Lake Tennessee 112
Lake Tiger 2,200
Lake Tracy 136
Lake Wales 326
Lake Weohyakapka 7,532
Lake Winterset 590

Sarasota County

Cow Pen Slough 170
Lower Myakka Lake 640
Myakka River 150
Upper Myakka Lake 1,020

St. Lucie County

Waterways 276

174

APPENDIX B

SOUTH FLORIDA COUNTY CHAMBERS OF COMMERCE

Brevard County
Melbourne Chamber of Commerce
1005 East Strawbridge Ave.
Melbourne, FL 32901
407/724-5400

Broward County
Ft. Lauderdale Chamber of Commerce
P.O. Box 14516
Fort Lauderdale, FL 33302
305/462-6000

Charlotte County
Port Charlotte Chamber of Commerce
2702 Tamiami Trail
Port Charlotte, FL 33952
813/627-2222

Collier County
Naples Area Chamber of Commerce
1700 North Tamiami Trail
Naples, FL 33940
813/262-6141

Dade County
Miami/Dade Convention
    & Visitors Bureau
701 Brickell Ave. #2700
Miami, FL 33131
800/283-2707

De Soto County
P.O. Box 149
Arcadia, FL 33821
813/494-4033

Glades County
P.O. Box 490
Moore Haven, FL 33471
813/946-0440

Hardee County
P.O. Box 683
Wauchula, FL 33873
813/773-6967

Hendry County
Clewiston Chamber of Commerce
P.O. Box 275
Clewiston, FL 33440
813/983-7979

Highlands County
Sebring Chamber of Commerce
309 South Circle
Sebring, FL 33870
813/385-8448

Indian River County
P.O. Box 2947
Vero Beach, FL 32961
407/567-3491

Lee County Convention
    & Visitors Bureau
P.O. Box 2445
Fort Myers, FL 33902
800/237-6444

Manatee County
P.O. Box 321
Bradenton, FL 34206
813/748-3411

Monroe County
Florida Keys Visitors Bureau
P.O. Box 866
Key West, FL 33041
800-FLA-KEYS

Okeechobee County
55 S. Parrott Ave.
Okeechobee, FL 33974
813/763-6464

Osceola County
Kissimmee/St. Cloud
    Convention & Visitors Bureau
P.O. Box 422007
Kissimmee, FL 34742
800/432-9199

Palm Beach County
    Convention & Visitors Bureau
1555 Palm Beach Lakes Blvd.
West Palm Beach, FL 33401
407/471-3995

Polk County Tourist
    Development Council
P.O. Box 1839
Bartow, FL 33830
813/534-4375

Sarasota County
P.O. Box 30
Sarasota, FL 34230
813/955-8187

St. Lucie County
2200 Virginia Ave.
Fort Pierce, FL 34982
407/461-2700

Game and Fresh Water Fish Commission
South Region, 3900 Drane Field Rd.,
Lakeland, FL 33811,
(813) 648-3202

Game and Fresh Water Fish Commission
Non-Native Fish Research,
801 N.W. 40th St.,
Boca Raton, FL 33431
(407) 391-6409.

Game and Fresh Water FishCommission
207 W. Carroll St.,
Kissimmee, FL 32741.

South Florida Water Management
    District,
Public Information Services,
3301 Gun Club Rod.,
West Palm Beach, FL 33402,
(305) 686-8800.

FISHING & HUNTING RESOURCE DIRECTORY

If you are interested in more productive fishing and hunting trips, then this info is for you!

Larsen's Outdoor Publishing is the publisher of several quality Outdoor Libraries - all informational-type books that focus on how and where to catch America's most popular sport fish, hunt popular and exciting big game, camp, dive or travel to exotic destinations.

The perfect-bound, soft-cover books include numerous illustrative graphics, line drawings, maps and photographs. The BASS SERIES LIBRARY as well as the HUNTING LIBRARIES are nationwide in scope. The INSHORE SERIES covers coastal areas from Texas to Maryland and foreign waters. The OUTDOOR TRAVEL SERIES and the OUTDOOR ADVENTURE LIBRARY cover the most exciting destinations in the world. The BASS WATERS SERIES focuses on the top lakes and rivers in the nation's most visited largemouth bass fishing state.

All series appeal to outdoorsmen/readers of all skill levels. The unique four-color cover design, interior layout, quality, information content and economical price makes these books hot sellers in the marketplace. Best of all, you can learn to be more successful in your outdoor endeavors!!

177

THE BASS SERIES LIBRARY
by Larry Larsen

1. FOLLOW THE FORAGE FOR BETTER BASS ANGLING VOL. 1 BASS/PREY RELATIONSHIP
Learn how to determine the dominant forage in a body of water, and you will consistently catch more and larger bass.

2. FOLLOW THE FORAGE FOR BETTER BASS ANGLING VOL. 2 TECHNIQUES
Learn why one lure or bait is more successful than others and how to use each lure under varying conditions.

3. BASS PRO STRATEGIES
Learn from the experience of the pros, how changes in pH, water temperature, color and fluctuations affect bass fishing, and how to adapt to weather and topographical variations.

4. BASS LURES - TRICKS & TECHNIQUES
Learn how to rig or modify your lures and develop specific presentation and retrieve methods to spark or renew the interest of largemouth!

5. SHALLOW WATER BASS
Learn specific productive tactics that you can apply to fishing in marshes, estuaries, reservoirs, lakes, creeks and small ponds. You'll likely triple your results!

6. BASS FISHING FACTS
Learn why and how bass behave during pre- and post-spawn, how they utilize their senses and how they respond to their environment, and you'll increase your bass angling success! This angler's guide to bass lifestyles and behavior is a reference source never before compiled.

7. TROPHY BASS
Take a look at geographical areas and waters that offer better opportunities to catch giant bass, as well as proven methods and tactics for man made/natural waters. "How to" from guides/trophy bass hunters.

8. ANGLER'S GUIDE TO BASS PATTERNS
Catch bass every time out by learning how to develop a productive pattern quickly and effectively. Learn the most effective combination of lures, methods and places for existing bass activity.

9. BASS GUIDE TIPS
Learn the most productive methods of top bass fishing guides in the country and secret techniques known only in a certain region or state that may work in your waters. Special features include shiners, sunfish kites & flies; flippin, pitchin' & dead stickin', rattlin', skippin' & jerk baits; deep, hot and cold waters; fronts, high winds & rain.

INSHORE SERIES
by Frank Sargeant

IL1. THE SNOOK BOOK
"Must" reading for anyone who loves the pursuit of this unique sub-tropic species. Every aspect of how you can find and catch big snook is covered.

IL2. THE REDFISH BOOK
Packed with expertise from the nation's leading redfish anglers and guides, this book covers every aspect of finding and fooling giant reds. You'll learn secret techniques revealed for the first time.

IL3. THE TARPON BOOK
Find and catch the wily "silver king" along the Gulf Coast, north through the mid-Atlantic, and south along Central and South American coastlines. Experts share their most productive techniques.

IL4. THE TROUT BOOK
You'll learn the best seasons, techniques and lures in this comprehensive book. Entertaining, informative reading for both the old salt and rank amateur.

BASS WATERS SERIES
by Larry Larsen

Take the guessing game out of your next bass fishing trip. The most productive bass water are described in this multi-volume series, plus ramp information, seasonal tactics, water characteristics and much more, including numerous maps and drawings and comprehensive index.

BW1. GUIDE TO NORTH FLORIDA BASS WATERS
From Orange Lake north and west.

BW2. GUIDE TO CENTRAL FLORIDA BASS WATERS
From Tampa/Orlando to Palatka.

BW3. GUIDE TO SOUTH FLORIDA BASS WATERS
From I-4 to the Everglades.

DEER HUNTING LIBRARY
by John E. Phillips

DH1. MASTERS' SECRETS OF DEER HUNTING
Increase your deer hunting success significantly by learning from the masters of the sport. New tactics and strategies.

DH2. THE SCIENCE OF DEER HUNTING
Specific ways to study the habits of deer to make your next scouting and hunting trips more successful. Learn the answers to many of the toughest deer hunting problems a sportsman ever encounters.

TURKEY HUNTING LIBRARY
by John E. Phillips

TH1. MASTERS' SECRETS OF TURKEY HUNTING
Masters of the sport have solved some of the most difficult problems you will encounter while hunting wily longbeardswith bows, blackpowder guns and shotguns.

OUTDOOR TRAVEL SERIES
by Timothy O'Keefe and Larry Larsen

Candid guides with vital recommendations that can make your next trip much more enjoyable.

OT1. FISH & DIVE THE CARIBBEAN - Volume 1
Northern Caribbean, including Cozumel, Caymans, Bahamas, Virgin Islands and other popular destinations.

OT3. FISH & DIVE FLORIDA & the Keys
Featuring fresh water springs; coral reefs; barrier islands; Gulf Stream/passes; inshore flats/channels and back country estuaries.

OUTDOOR ADVENTURE LIBRARY
by Vin Sparano

OA1. HUNTING DANGEROUS GAME
Know how it feels to face game that hunts back. You won't forget these classic tales of hunting adventures for grizzly, buffalo, lion, leopard, elephant, jaguar, wolves, rhinos and more!

Save Money on Your Next Outdoor Book!

Because you've purchased a Larsen's Outdoor Publishing
Book, you can be placed on our growing list of
preferred customers.

- You can receive special discounts on our wide selection
  of Bass Fishing, Saltwater Fishing, Hunting, Outdoor
  Travel and other economically-priced books written by
  our expert authors.

PLUS...

- **Receive Substantial Discounts for Multiple Book
  Purchases! And...advance notices on upcoming books!**

Send in your name TODAY to be added to our mailing list

_____ Yes, put my name on your mailing list to receive:

1. Advance notice on **upcoming outdoor books.**
2. Special **discount offers.**

Name_____

Address_____

City/State/Zip_____

**Send to: Larsen's Outdoor Publishing, Special Offers,
2640 Elizabeth Place, Lakeland, FL 33813**

LARSEN'S OUTDOOR PUBLISHING
CONVENIENT ORDER FORM
(All Prices Include Postage & Handling)

BASS SERIES LIBRARY - only $11.95 each - $79.95 autographed set

___ 1. Better Bass Angling - Vol. 1- Bass/Prey Interaction
___ 2. Better Bass Angling - Vol. 2 - Techniques
___ 3. Bass Pro Strategies
___ 4. Bass Lures - Tricks & Techniques
___ 5. Shallow Water Bass
___ 6. Bass Fishing Facts
___ 7. Trophy Bass
___ 8. Angler's Guide to Bass Patterns
___ 9. Bass Guide Tips

> **BIG SAVINGS!**
> Order 1 book, discount 5%
> 2-3 books, discount 10%.
> 4 or more books discount 20%.

INSHORE SERIES - only $11.95 each or $35.95 for autographed set

___ IL1. The Snook Book   ___ IL3. The Tarpon Book
___ IL2. The Redfish Book   ___ IL4. The Trout Book

BASS WATERS SERIES - only $14.95 each or $37.95 autographed set

___ BW1. Guide To North Florida Bass Waters
___ BW2. Guide To Central Florida Bass Waters
___ BW3. Guide to South Florida Bass Waters

BOOKS FROM OTHER SERIES- only $11.95 each

___ DH1. Masters' Secrets of Deer Hunting
___ DH2. The Science of Deer Hunting
___ TH1. Masters' Secrets of Turkey Hunting
___ OA1. Hunting Dangerous Game

OUTDOOR TRAVEL SERIES - only $13.95 each

___ OT1. Fish & Dive the Caribbean Vol 1 - Northern Caribbean
___ OT3. Fish & Dive Florida & the Keys

NAME _____

ADDRESS_____

CITY_____STATE_____ZIP_____

No. of books ordered _____ x $_____ each = _____
No. of books ordered _____ x $_____ each = _____
            Multi-bookDiscount (%)   = _____
TOTAL ENCLOSED (Check or Money Order) $_____

Copy this page and mail to:
Larsen's Outdoor Publishing,
2640 Elizabeth Place, Lakeland, FL 33813

WRITE US!

By the way, if your books have helped you be more productive in your outdoor endeavors, we'd like to hear from you. Let us know which book or series has strongly benefitted you and how it has aided your success or enjoyment.

We might be able to use the information in a future book. Such information is also valuable to our planning future titles and expanding on those already available.

Simply write to: Larry Larsen, Publisher, Larsen's Outdoor Publishing, 2640 Elizabeth Place, Lakeland, Fl 33813.

We appreciate your comments!

INDEX

I

J

K

L